CREEKCRAFT

CREEK
William C. Black
CRAFT

THE ART OF FLYFISHING
SMALLER STREAMS

PRUETT P PUBLISHING COMPANY
Boulder, Colorado

First Edition
1 2 3 4 5 6 7 8 9

Library of Congress Cataloging-in-Publication Data

Black, William C., 1931-
   Creek craft: the art of flyfishing smaller streams / by
William C. Black.
      p.   cm.
   Bibliography: p.
   ISBN 0-87108-747-2 (pbk.)
   1. Fly fishing.   I. Title.
SH456.B54 1988
799.1'2 — dc19   88-23443
                                          CIP

Designed by Jody Chapel, Cover to Cover Design,
Denver, Colorado.

Contents

The Fascination of Small Streams

Diminutive troutstreams hold a particular intimate charm. These fisheries can hardly hide many secrets. Their banks, their beds, and the very lifeblood of their flow are all close at hand. For the angler there is a sense of belonging along a small stream as if he were a transient part of its fauna. When plying a yawning river I feel like a visitor, tolerated perhaps, but a guest nonetheless. Those of us who cut our fishing teeth on small streams feel indebted too for lessons learned combined with pleasant memories. It's a mistake to assume that liberties can be taken with a pretty brook or that its conquest will be easy.

The reason small streams are special hinges upon the physical relationships between a narrow ribbon of water and the banks containing it. As a stream's width and depth decrease there is a corresponding reduction in the scale of its internal parts. Pools, riffles, currents, and eddies all shrink proportionately. Compared to a broad river, a creek is like a dollhouse with tiny rooms and miniature furniture. Meanwhile the anglers who play there—and more critically the shrubs, trees, and boulders along its banks—remain full size. Tall conifers that are nothing more than a decorative fringe along a broad river virtually smother a timid brook. A rim of willows is a mere afterthought on a river, but that same vegetation may canopy a more modest stream, shutting out sun and sky. If a major stream's banks are steep and bluffy beyond the high-water line, that will

hardly matter: the angler can make his way along a strip of open shore. Those same bluffs brought close to a creek mean a canyon that will be rough to negotiate.

This cheek-by-jowl relationship between small streams and their containers influences the fishing. On narrow streams the angler must deal with the problem of "enforced proximity." Proximity equates with closeness, often of an uncomfortable degree, between fishermen and trout. Bank structure does most of the enforcing. Casting is more difficult, since things that stick up and out from banks, whether trees, bushes, or barbed wire fences, have a way of catching flies. Wading up the middle and casting parallel to the banks could be a solution except that creeks love to bend and twist, making throws of any length impractical. A second and equally troublesome aspect is the threat of spooking the fish as you move along. It's desirable to stay in or very close to the water in order to see how things are laid out. The bind comes when you suddenly find yourself right on top of a piece of excellent target water, so close that it's likely spoiled. Walking the banks well back from the edge is safer, but what if they're thickly overgrown or too steep? Then it's back into the water. This is why stalking skills are so critical for the small stream fisherman. Special casts are necessary too. Some are just modifications of standard techniques designed to cheat obstructions, whereas others are less traditional means of propelling a fly in tight quarters. Although Nature makes things tough at times, there are ways to cope, and this is part of the fun in creekcraft.

But what is a *small* stream? One thing's certain, the map names "river" and "creek" as labels for large as opposed to small won't do as definition boundaries. Stream naming is decidedly regional and, at times, frivolous. In the parched Southwest we are much given to bragging. Here we have rivers, so named, whose sandy beds sparkle in the bright sun and others that can be cleared via a standing broadjump. At higher latitudes up in the wetter Rockies and in the Northwest things are different. There you'll find mighty streams that a major league outfielder couldn't throw a stone across hiding behind the skirts of the bashful appellation "creek." Some years ago I got quite a shock while fishing the Wind River below Dubois, Wyoming. The combination of a late runoff plus heavy rain had pretty much ruined the Wind. Our host at the Cross Mill Iron Ranch offered to ask if we might fish the "crick" on his brother's property across the fence line. After walking just a few minutes, I assumed that we had taken the wrong trail that led back to the river, for we heard the roar of heavy water echoing through a stand of cottonwoods. Breaking into the open on a high bank, I still wasn't sure. The stream below looked navigable for ships up to destroyer class. It certainly wasn't fordable. Still, looking eastward some quarter of a mile, there lay the great, grey Wind River, some four times larger! As it turned out, we were standing on the bank of little old Dinwoody Creek, a "megacreek" to say the least.

Getting back to "small," adjectives are difficult to define because they describe qualities which are relative. A working definition is clearly the best, provided it's also realistic. I look at how specific channel width correlates with enforced proximity. On the basis of many years of rod-to-brush combat I offer the following generalization: It seems that as a stream's average width expands beyond about 30 feet, the constraints and difficulties brought about by the fencing qualities of bank structure begin to fade as practical considerations. There is more freedom beyond 30 feet or so in terms of options in the choice of casting positions and also more variation in the kinds of casts that might be attempted. You also have an opportunity to pick routes in or along the water with lessened threat of frightening the fish. In essence, there is more breathing room. By contrast, on the other side of this 10-yard width the ability to throw short, precise casts becomes increasingly essential. So does stalking.

Let me emphasize that there is nothing concrete about the 30-foot break point. For one thing, creeks breathe in and out as they flow along, as if provided

Cloistered in a narrow canyon.

The same stream in a meadow affords elbow room.

with elastic waistbands. A stream with an average width of 25 feet is quite capable of sucking it in to 15 feet or letting out its belly to 40 feet. Thus, some segments fish small whereas others offer the relaxation of greater width. Further, as you can readily imagine, a creek with flattish banks uncluttered by trees, tall shrubs, etc. is going to fish bigger than its width would suggest. Where fencing-in is not a factor, a good deal of stalking and casting can be accomplished from dry land with all of the extra freedom that this implies. It is for these reasons that the 30-foot definition can be only an approximation.

After so much discussion of enforced proximity, casting hangups, and spooked trout, small-stream fishing sounds more like penance than pleasure. It's not. Beyond the opportunity to catch lots of fish, there is an aesthetic side. Little streams are private places. An angler can easily become addicted to a particular favorite, returning time and again, until he comes to regard it as his own. I have experienced flashes of totally unreasonable anger upon finding another person working a piece of "my water." A creek of this sort can become a kind of individual retreat, a sanctuary for contemplation and restoration of the spirit, a font of peace of mind. A good deal of the lasting pleasure derived from fishing has to do with happy memories involving a special experience in a specific place along a stream. It seems that images formed on small water are sharpest. It's hard to forget that submerged tree limb overgrown with moss where the big brown trout appeared to take your fly or the small pool pocked by a rise during a November snow flurry. Small stream detail, reduced as it is in scale, is especially sharply etched. Coarser, big-water features seem blurred around the edges in memory.

Beyond this the flyfisher learns to anticipate the proximity to nature that close-set banks necessarily entail. The margins of a brook are busy with wildflowers and bird and animal life. Their contribution to the ambience of a fishing time and place, to the appreciation of the experience of a day, must be felt. I know a pair of friendly water ouzels whose canyon home I share on occasion. It's pleasant to fantasize that they remember me. They faithfully flit and dart along, watching my antics, all the while dipping comically up and down as if amused. (They may be.)

The prospect of temporarily withdrawing from society is only part of the attraction that small streams hold. There are more practical considerations, such as the fact that minor flystreams are more numerous than large ones. It has to be that way. Topographically restricted basins such as those in high mountains can't spawn flows of much magnitude. Neither can more spacious areas of semiarid terrain. Further, major drainage systems supporting a full-fledged river almost always offer secondary tributary streams. Although I live in Albuquerque, a sizable city in an arid state, there are still a number of pretty creeks that I can reach and return from within part of a single day. The nearest big water is by no means so accessible. The storied Box Canyon of the Rio Grande up north by Taos is a three-hour drive to the edge of a cavernous gorge. The long, billy-goat trail down becomes much longer still on the way home. New Mexico's other blue ribbon troutery, the San Juan River below Navajo Dam, is a four-hour drive one way. So unless I have a couple of days at my disposal, it's either a matter of plying the nearby creeks or not going at all.

Even if you are in the neighborhood of a river, there may be reasons to fish its tributaries. During early season runoff the big stream can be in such spate that it is unfishable while less rambunctious feeder streams offer good sport. The same is true when summer cloudbursts wash so much mud into rivers that even the bait boys are discouraged. Often sources of this roil are just trickle tributaries or dry arroyos with eroded banks, yet in this situation it's common for more significant feeder creeks to remain clear. Then there are those exciting tributaries with spawning runs of good fish coming up from a river or lake. There are days, too, when we simply wish to get away from roads and people, concentrated as they predictably will be along the big stream. It's also quite possible that fishing will be better on "less improved" tributaries.

Like it or not, pernicious shrinkage of available trout water is a fact of life for most of us. As our population has grown with increasing demands for water, fishing has become more rather than less popular. Add in pollution in its various forms and you have a collision phenomenon in a very real sense. The result is the subtraction of parts or all of certain streams from our places to fish. One resulting piece of sociological shrapnel has been the leasing of private water to groups or clubs whose fees often discourage the average angler. There is a disturbingly long list of ranches in Colorado and Wyoming that I once enjoyed fishing on a pay-for-trespass basis that are off-limits today, probably forever. These factors work in concert to reduce our options. Now and then a bit of new water becomes available, as below a dam on a river too warm or silty to sustain trout, but these tailwater fisheries can't begin to balance the books for those of us who prefer running water. The bottom line is clear enough: we must expand our vistas as to where we will fish. So as the old song goes, your piscatorial happiness may indeed come to lie within your own backyard.

I do not mean to imply that all small trout streams are alike. The diversity of minor streams is perhaps their most entertaining feature. The nature of a creek's bed, the quantities and types of insect life it contains, the velocity of its current and shape of its channel are all critical. In mountainous terrain elevation matters. Relative accessibility is always important as measured by the "beercan index." This can indicate how easy or difficult a place is to get at and hence the level of competition expected. All of these features and others too fit into a complexly-interrelated ecosystem that determines the fishing qualities of a given stream. When you consider the various possibilities and variables, the permutations and combinations suggest the need for computerization. At one time I even contemplated a means for cataloging streams into types. I gave up, confused by overlapping, fuzzy definitions. I'm glad. Some things, a few at least, are better left uncomputerized.

Small and unpretentious streams are easily overlooked by the angling public. This presents the intriguing possibility of ferreting out little known yet productive fisheries. I know a trickle so tiny in a canyon so steep that no one in his right mind would bother with it. I've had a lot of fun there. Van-size rocks in the crotch of the canyon bully the creeklet about unmercifully. Beyond forming pools, where the boulders lie, vegetation can't protrude. Thus there are little pockets of space for casts along the faces and summits of the big rocks. And the trout in this canyon have never heard of fishermen. Their mothers never told them. As you can imagine,

there is mutual excitement when a 14-inch brownie in some bathtub of a pool feels your hook! Getting up this staircase of a canyon is much like completing an obstacle course. It's a good place for breaking rod tips, and you'll likely come out with some scratches and bruises. One day I was actually torpedoed while wading around a rocky ledge. My composure was shattered by a loud, percussive splash close by my elbow. Recoiling instinctively, I saw a dark form streak toward my knee. A solid bump and "it" was gone. I presume (and hope) that the thing was a beaver into whose home I had stumbled. I don't know if his paws shook for the next few minutes, but my hands certainly did.

This canyon reminds me of a blunt question once posed to me by a fellow angler: "You're an experienced fisherman...why do you fuss with those little streams?" Skipping what I saw as some important aesthetics, I simply replied that there is satisfaction and enjoyment in learning to do a difficult set of things well. I'm sure he didn't understand, and that may be just as well. I've seen many egos wounded and tempers lost along small streams. Creekcraft is that way.

2
Reading Small Water

COVER

HOLDING

FOOD

FLAT WATER

WINTER

PRE-RUNOFF

RUNOFF

SUBSIDING RUNOFF

SUMMER

FALL COOL-DOWN

Reading Small Water

"Reading the water" is the essence of stream fishing. I don't know who first compared reading water to reading print, but the comparison is apt. Just as sentences are made up of words, and words of letters, so is stream detail composed of coarser and finer pieces. A sentence takes its meaning from the units contained within. A stream is read in much the same way. The angler visually separates individual pieces of water each from its neighbors. This sorting out process is based on the premise that different parts of a stream will demonstrate varying levels of fishing merit. Certain pieces have an excellent chance of containing interested trout, others are less likely bets, whereas still others will probably prove unresponsive to an angler's solicitations.

Breaking a stream up into zones on the basis of fishing potential is eminently practical. If the "printed stream" is read accurately, a great deal of time and effort can be saved. It's the familiar Willie Sutton principle. Willie chose to rob banks because "that's where the money was." Water reading translates into fundamental decisions as to which pieces of water are to be fished carefully, which are to be skipped, the choice of casting positions, and so forth. Until you have identified and prioritized target areas, you have no base from which to initiate operations. Everything has to begin with reading unless you are prepared to beat the whole stream nonselectively. This is something successful fishermen never do.

Water reading is pretty much the same no matter the size of a stream. Small streams are nonetheless distinctive. The structural detail upon which reading depends is more sharply defined in more diminutive streams. Although detail is close-set and jumbled to form a busy set of sentences, the structure is still there to be read. And importantly, the angler is right on top of the page. Even fine print is easy to see at close range. As a result small streams make outstanding schools for the beginner. Happily, the lessons learned can also be applied in several ways to big water where detail is often ambiguous.

I begin with the assumption that trout also break their watery environment into pieces and parts. Their position in the stream is clearly a matter of choice, and they surely don't distribute themselves randomly. I separate these qualities into three categories: The first is *cover*, portions of the stream where trout will be protected from danger. The second is *holding*. Despite their streamlined (sorry) forms and slick skins, trout must expend energy to maintain a position in current. Holding water is reasonably slow, permitting conservation of energy. The third is *food*, because certain portions of a stream will be richer than others. Unfortunately, it's not possible to list cover, holding, and food in order of importance because that will change with the conditions at hand.

Cover

Features offering cover value can be characterized as follows:

1. Physical objects that protrude into the water from the stream's bed or banks.
2. Discolored water, i.e., less than clear.
3. A riffled or choppy surface.
4. Deeper water.
5. Patches of shade.

Physical cover objects include rocks from hat size up to boulders, submerged tree limbs, beds of water weed, steep bank faces, etc. I have even seen trout rise from the shelter of a discarded truck tire. Nor do trout necessarily require an object that they can get under — a vertical rock face or steep bank will do. It's also important to realize that physical features sufficient to provide sanctuary for several fish can be of unimpressive dimensions. Creeks are typically cluttered with all sorts of cover structure.

Whereas objects may provide cover, the whole stream shows the same degree of clarity. This can set a sort of mood among the trout. When the water is roily and semiopaque, trout may become bold, ranging freely and feeding in water that would otherwise provide little safety. Conversely, when gin-clear conditions obtain, the fish are much more prone to be suspicious and skittish, seeking out lies with the best protection. The angler needs to adjust his reading accordingly.

One of the oldest theories in angling involves the so-called "window" through which fish look up and out on the terrestrial world. This is an oval area in the surface film over the trout's head. "Window" is an appropriate term because the optical physics of the surface film beyond the margins of the oval cause the film to function not as a window, but as a mirror, reflecting the bottom. The crux is that for the window to be transparent for the fish, the surface must be smooth. Otherwise the window area too becomes a dancing daze of tiny mirrors. What does this mean for the trout? Surely they ought to feel more secure when they can see out through their window. However, a choppy surface is a two-way street. It also obscures underwater objects (such as fish) as viewed from above the water. So while trout probably see poorly through a rough surface film, they are also hidden from threats from above. Trout seem to perceive a choppy surface as a cover feature, for they often feed contentedly in a bouncy riffle over a flat and otherwise exposed streambed. Small, swift streams have lots of surface chop and hence another sort of cover detail.

We can only guess as to why fish appear to feel safer in deeper water. As with a rough surface it may be that their concern involves predators that might dive for them, such as kingfishers, osprey, mergansers, and mink. Perhaps a thicker layer of water affords extra protection? According to biologists, a trout's window enlarges with increasing depth. The farther submerged, the more of the outside world he sees. This depth aspect is one example of why creeks are easier to read than rivers. Let's guess that a depth of three feet is likely enough to satisfy these instincts for preservation and that much of a certain river meets this requirement. In this case depth *per se* is not going to be a very useful reading feature. But take a creek that has only a few pools as deep as three feet, say only 2 percent of the surface area. These pools will naturally be more important, and so will pieces of water that are only 24 inches thick. In shallow streams like this, the trout are delighted to accept a thinner layer of water over their backs as pretty fair cover. So relative depth becomes a valuable reading aid when there isn't a lot of it to go around.

A patch of shade offers sanctuary of a sort and may be cast by objects such as a streambed boulder or high bank to yield double cover value. Here we see another contrast between the creek and the river. Creeks are consistently dappled with shadows cast by bankside vegetation, whereas this kind of cover is restricted to the very margins of broad rivers.

Holding

Reading for holding quality has its subtleties, too. In many instances cover objects also create holding. Things that protrude into currents from the bed or banks act as deflectors that create zones of quieter water on their downstream sides. In *The Ecology of Running*

Waters[1] Hynes shows an interesting diagram and photograph of a stream of flowing cellulose acetate particles passing through a tube and over a rounded object that simulates a streambed rock. This object deflects the current in a way that you can actually see because the cellulose particles are visible in the strobe-lighted photograph. The reader can see an image of both current velocity and direction of flow. Along the downstream face of the "rock," the current stream slows, becomes turbulent, and portions of it reverse direction, beginning to backflow. You can convince yourself that deflectors actually work by reaching behind a modest rock sticking up into the current. You can feel the size and shape of the area of altered or muted flow. You may be surprised at how much of a window in the current a smallish rock or other structure can create. It's the same way with steep bank faces of uneven contour. It doesn't take much to wedge out a window of holding large enough to satisfy a trout or two.

STREAM OF PARTICLES

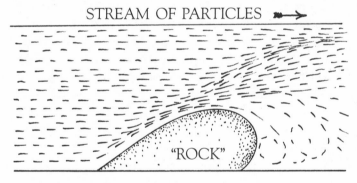

Deflectors break the current's thrust.

One of the complexities in reading for holding and cover is that neither is an all-or-none phenomenon. There are in-between quantities such as the knot of willow roots that gets credit for a little cover and a little holding value, the current that is neither swift nor slow, water that is slightly murky, or a depth that's intermediate. A single feature may also create opposite cover and holding qualities. For instance, strong currents usually create a choppy surface, leading to a poor holding/good cover mix. Slack water means good holding, but its surface is typically slick. Unless other factors such as depth enter in, the reciprocal mixture of

good holding/poor cover will apply. In circumstances such as these you'll have to decide which quality is the more important on the basis of supply and demand. It's pretty certain that the trout will prize most whichever quality is in the shortest supply. When water levels are high and currents pound and tear, holding will be more valued. At the opposite extreme, when streams are low they are also usually clear and smooth. Cover needs will be dominant in that situation.

Food

At first glance correlating stream structure with food content could be difficult. It might seem that food should be quite spread out within a stream. Victuals, however, are concentrated by *currents*. No matter how edibles get into the water, they are awash and drifting. Currents concentrate drifting food, since a current consists of a large volume of water passing through a restricted area. A strip of moving water literally acts as a funnel. But here is another contradiction in reading values, holding versus food content. From the trout's viewpoint I suppose currents must be watery structures at crossed purposes. Some sort of tradeoff is necessary. Trout don't mind though; they're good at tradeoffs. To begin, there's no reason that they must seek food in the strongest currents. Lesser flows will concentrate edibles too, if in lesser amounts. If a good deal of fodder happens to be awash, the minor currents may offer a bargain in terms of energy expenditure. Current systems also change velocity over space. They build quickly at the head or upstream end as minor currents coalesce. The midportion or spine of the current will have the most muscle. Then comes the tail. Current tails spread and fan out, losing force. Going back to the funnel analogy, note that most of the water that was gathered at the head comes out to form the tail, like a funnel's spout. Trout feed regularly in caressing current tails. Don't give up on the strongest or gut portion of the channel though. If the bottom is rocky and jagged the fish may have their cake and eat it too. Streambeds can be as sawtoothed as miniature mountain ranges. The valleys and crevasses between the rugged summits are protected from the rip of the current while the food it carries zips right by the

[1] H. B. N. Hynes, *The Ecology of Running Waters* (Toronto: University of Toronto Press, 1970), p. 8.

mountain peaks. Trout love to lie in wait down in those valleys. Another nice thing about smaller streams is that current beds are usually plainly visible from close range. You can tell whether the bottom is smooth with little holding or jagged and hence more promising.

Current edges are prevalent, obvious, and very valuable reading symbols. The theme is the same as with the submerged mountain range, i.e., rapid flow abutting slower water. There's an analogy to real estate wherein the value of a piece of property is much influenced by adjacent features such as a major highway or the ocean front. You can see that the strip of water just off the current's edge picks up good marks by its proximity to a pipeline of food.

A pretty feeding current sweeps a grassy bank. Note the tiny wavelets.

There is one prime form of food-enriched water that has been called a feeding current or feeding riffle. These currents appear to have fair thrust when in reality they tumble and percolate along without much push. The trout tell us that feeding riffles are full of food, for these are predictably the highest yield pieces of target water you can find. I think of feeding riffles as current ricochets. They may form below the intersection of two currents that merge at an angle or where a tongue of swift flow bounces off a rock's face. An especially common location is alongside the necks of major runs where merging currents collect strength, pitching downward over a rocky bed. Look for surface chop made up of tiny wavelets in a somewhat regular pattern. There is an impression of a monotonous set of miniature waves, each about equidistant from its neighbors with the long axis of each tiny crest running crosswise to the direction of flow.

We've considered several situations in which trout are able to avail themselves of current-borne food while expending as little energy as possible. However, when the price is right, poor holding is not much of a factor. Given an opportunity to fill their stomachs, trout will tackle the toughest of currents. Hour by hour the available quantities of food fluctuate far more than do cover and holding. A hatch or mating swarm of insects can load currents with provender over a period of just a few minutes. Or a little wind might blow numbers of grasshoppers or other terrestrial food into the water from the banks. These periods of plenty are often quite brief, and when they do occur, the trout are likely to gorge themselves. If an abundance of calorie-rich fodder is channeling down, they can afford to buck the punishing thrust. Their intake of fuel exceeds the amount burned in the effort.

You will also see acceptance of poor cover when the prize is food. Certain nymphs such as those of the dragonfly clamber onto rocks and reed stems along the banks like buggy landing craft in the process of hatching. Trout sometimes expose their dorsal fins during frantic pursuit through bankside shoals. Brownies in particular have a habit of slumming in the shallows. Most often the payoff is an easy shot at terrestrials that hop, fly, fall, or otherwise get into the creek. Thus pieces of apparently mediocre water against a bank sometimes produce major surprises. Because so much of a small stream's flow is against the banks, the importance of these bankside strips is magnified.

Slumming in the shoals.

Flat Water

Flat water is so commonplace in freestone streams as to pass notice. Flat water is typically brisk, reasonably shallow, and flows across a bed of rocks. In short it's the kind of stream detail that fills in the gaps between runs and pools. Nonetheless, the ability to read flat water is critical. Flat water holds many more fish than its nondescript nature might suggest, but because its detail is minute, this kind of stream structure is difficult to read. As a consequence, a sizable proportion of the fishing public neither appreciates nor is able to take advantage of the flat parts of streams. This is not an elitist flyfisher's view, but hard fact. Also, baits and spinning lures tend to run aground in flat water. This means that those anglers will prefer to fish pools and deeper runs.

Flat-water detail is subtle, but the trout are there.

The fisherman who ignores flat water pays a variety of penalties. There are good streams that are simply poor in pools. Fishing the pools also means working the hardest-hit parts of a stream. Aside from becoming depleted of trout, there's always a good chance that someone has been through a pool only minutes before you, leaving its inhabitants in a temporary state of chaos. Pools can also produce poorly for no apparent reason. This has happened to me many times in wilderness settings when I knew I was alone and trout were plentiful. I've thought that perhaps the fish who live in the elegance of these posh places are more selective than their brethren out on the flat water streets of the stream. Whatever, I can't count the times when the ragamuffin flat water has outproduced the pretty, deep green places.

How to decipher flat water? The first step is to learn to recognize greatly scaled-down versions of full-size pools—miniature replicas. A "mini-pool" that would fit into a bathtub or even a washbasin has the same anatomical parts as a full-grown pool. The feeding current may be more like a faucet's flow, and the deep center will probably be measured in inches rather than in feet.

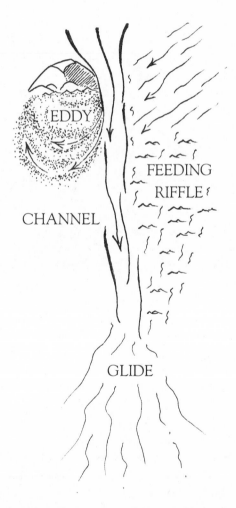

Small pools have the same components as large pools, such as a central channel, eddies, riffles, and glides.

No matter, to the trout a pool is a pool. Tiny pools called rock pockets are often formed by surfacing stones. The rock creates a small piece of holding and offers a little cover while accelerating slips of flow to either side collect a little food. Rock pockets are natural inhabitants of small streams, and this is one reason why creeks are such good reading schools. The next step is to try to find submerged rock pockets. The least subtle are formed by the kind of stones that stick up enough above the creekbed to trip you while wading. Eventually you'll be able to spot lesser current deflectors that raise their heads just a little above neighboring stones. There is great satisfaction in seeing a trout come from one of these occult holds to take your fly.

Earlier I suggested that lessons learned on small streams are helpful in unravelling the secrets of big rivers where structural contrasts are so often blurred. Between Quake Lake and Ennis, Montana, the Madison River is essentially a 50-mile ribbon of flat water. The current is uniformly swift over a bed of rounded stones. On the occasion of my maiden visit to the Madison I came armed with a detailed map drawn by my wife's uncle Hank. Prior to the terrible earthquake of 1959, Hank owned a fishing camp on what is now the bed of Quake Lake, and he knew the Madison intimately. Hank had touted me to a particular "hole" where he routinely got into multi-pound fish. My map showed that I was to turn off the Varney Bridge road on the east bank along a rough track, drive a certain distance, and find a stack of salt blocks. Then I was to line up that stack with the top of a grove of tall cottonwoods on the far bank. It was just like *Treasure Island*. The treasure was located on that line near the center of the river. Everything went smoothly until I reached the bank. Then my excitement quickly changed to frustration. I could see no sign of any sort of hole. Worse, I hadn't a clue as to how to read the Madison. Within several hundred yards there were only three or four boulders breaking surface. Otherwise the bottom looked like a bad cobblestone street covered by a sheet of water of virtually uniform velocity and depth. I searched all morning and into the afternoon for that "hole." I retraced my steps, looked for another stack of salt blocks and another grove of cottonwoods. No dice. Eventually it dawned on me that I needed to read the Madison for fine detail as if it were

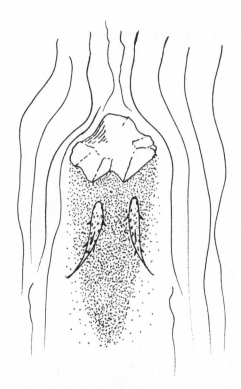

Rock pockets are really tiny pools.

a giant creek. So despite the hugeness of my surroundings, I began to pretend. I think I finally found the hole, for the best two fish of the day came from a spot along the map's line. It certainly wasn't a piece of water that jumped out and bit you, though. A cluster of largish rocks on the riverbed apparently diverted the current, causing it to scoop out an elongate, shallow depression. This strip wasn't over 50 feet in length and was carpeted by gravel and small stones. I'd guess that some combination of good holding quality and swirling, food-laden current must have attracted the hefty rainbows.

There's another chapter in this textbook of transposed reading skills. Rivers can intimidate when dangerously swift and obscure of detail. They make me feel small and overmatched. Regardless, water must meet land at some point along the margin of every stream, large or small. They all have exactly two banks. Fortunately water along the banks is very likely to be slower and shallower than in the main channel and to display far more physical detail. Food enters from terra firma too, so this narrow strip is truly angler-friendly. For me there is a welcome feeling of familiarity when working the banks of even the most monstrous rivers. It's as if

I were fishing a one-sided, smaller stream. Trout appreciate banksides too, even along the biggest rivers. When you think of a river's margin as a one-banked creek, the reading skills learned on small water apply nicely. So once again the creek becomes the classroom for the river.

Seasonal changes are among flyfishing's most fascinating accents. Although the calendar doesn't alter the basics of water reading, the message contained and the way in which the information is used by the angler are highly sensitive to seasonal influences. Changes in water level, temperature, and clarity are particularly evident on smaller streams.

Winter

With water temperatures in the low 30s, it's a biological reality that the cold-blooded trout's metabolism gets turned way down. With their motors barely idling there is little need to forage for food. Other life in the stream will have become dormant too. It would be folly for the frigid fish to range about in barren currents, expending energy. Typically the trout gravitate to the deep, still pools. They "hole up." Even the pretty pockets are deserted as snowbanks bridge out to join caps of white on boulders in the channel. Where the flow is slower, surface ice thickens, while a glacial sheet, creeping along the creekbed, sandwiches the remaining water. These igloo quarters must be too tight for comfort. Winter water reading is remedial: Fish the pools!

Last January the bleakness of it all got the best of me. I made a token appearance at work and by noon found myself on a nearby creek with gloves, thermal socks, and long johns. Immersing the barrel of my thermometer, I felt strange little ticks as if the glass rod were breaking. Looking closely I saw that shards of ice, the barest slivers, were drifting against the barrel like tiny icebergs. The column read 31 degrees! I couldn't believe my eyes, although biologists say that super cooling is possible in swiftly flowing water. I thought about heading back, but here was a chance to set a new personal record for foolishness. Sheets of ice shattered against my boots as I pushed along through the shallows, giving the sensation of wading through dry cornflakes. Yet would you believe that in a couple of hours I caught

four trout on a streamer? The browns were so stiff and stick-like I was afraid the poor things might break as they flopped feebly on the snow. Every fish I saw that day was holed up in the deep slack of a sizable pool. They still weren't in total hibernation though, even at one degree below freezing.

One of the nicest things about cold-weather fishing is that there won't be anyone around to disturb the silence. It's a stillness that complements the beauty of dynamic snow-and-ice formations sculpted by passing currents. Besides, a torpid trout or two seems quite enough when you know there are things you should be doing back at home. Having a small stream close enough for these occasional outings makes the winter go by faster.

Pre-runoff

Before the arrival of spring there is an interesting phase in the angling year that correlates with longer, warmer days. Snow recedes from the banks at lower elevations and in open places as water temperatures climb out of the numbing 30s into the frigid 40s during afternoons. The amount of melt won't be nearly as heavy as later, and streams are typically full rather than high. They often remain fairly clear as well. While still pretty much holed up, the trout begin to show signs of awakening feeding interest. You'll find them creeping furtively into the very best pieces of water near their winter lies, perhaps the edge of an eddy or a feeding riffle. Just a little warming helps to light the pilots of their metabolic furnaces. If it's only the pilot, a few fish are still likely to take a shot at passing food. For whatever reason I occasionally catch surprisingly large trout during the pre-runoff.

Reading the water is still straightforward. In addition to the deep pools you'll want to try adjacent prime pieces of water, skipping swift currents, pockets, and marginal targets. Cover should be plentiful, so you can work at close range. I like to think of the pre-runoff as a specific phase. Otherwise it's easy to forget this part of the season and to miss some pretty fair fishing.

The pre-runoff brings solitude, beauty . . . and an occasional trout.

Runoff

The definitive runoff is a period of violent excess. Bullying currents bash and scour the streamcourse as if it were being mugged. The trout have no recourse but to seek whatever holding they can find. And with multiplying flow comes roily, opaque water. Trout are not eager to play blind man's bluff, ranging about for food they can't see. Meanwhile snowmelt keeps the lid on water temperatures despite warming weather. Thus do the components of the runoff work in concert against the angler.

The magnitude and power of a rambunctious runoff is startling. Small streams in particular are vulnerable to remarkable variations in flow. During a heavy runoff the volume may be six to eight times that of midsummer and over twenty times the flow observed during low water periods in the fall. A mere brook in which children wade on a summer picnic may have been too much for the most intrepid fisherman to cross only two months earlier. The tremendous disruption of the spate of spring is especially evident to the small-stream angler through the magnifying effects of proximity. When a big, unwadable river rises a foot or so, it's still just that, a big unwadable river. A change of similar magnitude on a creek's scale will easily double its width and depth.

Normal bank structures disappear altogether as the channel becomes a surge of icy brown. As to fishing during the full-bore runoff, I don't!

Subsiding Runoff

Although the raucous effluents of winter may virtually run us out of our favorite creeks, the receding runoff promises some of the most exciting sport of the entire year. Watch for an abrupt reversal of fishing fortunes as a couple of factors begin to work in the angler's favor. It's logical that the trout will want to get back to the business of feeding after their long fast. This is triggered in part by rising temperatures and clearing water. As stream levels begin to normalize, holding is more plentiful too.

The real catalyst, though, is food. A parallel burst of activity is ongoing within the insect world. Nymphs destined to hatch or molt become active while the many creatures that inhabit banks reappear. The stream and its banks come into bloom along with the rest of the countryside. To huddle sedentarily in winter holding places would be to ignore the plentiful food borne in currents and the more stationary delectables such as larvae clinging precariously to rocks or nymphs crawling dangerously across the bottom rubble. Many of the important mayfly hatches occur in early season. Caddis make their contribution, and in the West the stone fly is apt to occupy center stage. This is why trout come to the table in hungry droves as the runoff loses its punch.

The fading runoff is tricky nonetheless. It takes much less stream change than you might think to turn the trout on. I've been fooled on many an occasion by a chilly, swollen creek that looked inhospitable only to find its inhabitants feeding aggressively. Although holding is still in short supply and hence an important reading specific, ravenous trout may be foraging in currents or hanging just off the face of a powerful flow. Thus the still depths that you worked earlier may no longer produce as well as currents.

Summer

The trout will have spread out to occupy every nook and cranny that suits their fancy to include the flat water. Increasing quantities of food are entering from the banks. Holding is much less critical than earlier, while cover is more so. The importance of each of the three reading parameters comes into more even balance during summer. All is stable unless heavy rains come along to recreate the high water and murk of the runoff.

Fall Cool-Down

The backside of the flyfisher's year is much smoother than the front. As days and nights grow cooler, water temperatures follow suit. October's weather may be bright and blue, but stream thermometer readings are going to dip progressively with assists from early snows in the high country. The first hint of a shift in trout distribution will be a falloff in action in smaller pockets and flat water. Thus begins a pattern of withdrawal toward holed-up status that continues over several months. This doesn't mean that late-season fishing will be poor. There's no question that the degree of fish dispersal within a stream and the trout's willingness to feed are basically separate issues. There are many streams

in which fishing is far better in the cool of Indian Summer than during the summer months. At both ends of the season the water will be at its warmest during the afternoons before too much sun has left the stream. Trout sometimes appear to be holed up early in the day and yet lesser, flat-water targets produce nicely later on. A creek may come "un-holed" as the day progresses. Perhaps the fish were lying in these shallow targets all along, waiting for their thermostats to be tripped. Or possibly they move out of deeper holding as conditions improve.

If I were granted just one wish that would apply to fishing, I'd ask for the ability to accurately predict the beginning and duration of these various phases for any given stream. It would take some magic because so many factors impact on stream conditions. Some, such as latitude, the elevation of the drainage, and average precipitation for the region are stable. These you can figure, more or less. The rest, however, amounts to a meteorologic crapshoot. The preceding winter's snowpack is certainly a potent consideration. The same is obviously true for the more recent weather. A meagre snowpack means a runty runoff with the early advent of good flyfishing unless the spring is cold and wet. Conversely, a stretch of warm, dry weather, hard on winter's heels, will release the heaviest snowpack, creating a violent but brief runoff. I've made a hobby out of guessing about stream conditions during the cracks between the major seasons, especially in the spring. This gives me the best chance to plan my fishing time to coincide with the most promising conditions. Part of this game involves keeping a log in which dates, snowpacks, weather, and the status of individual streams are recorded year by year. It's an entertaining and practical pastime. Reservoirs with controlled outflow give you another unknown to ponder. When part of the excess of the runoff is held back to fill the impoundment, a reservoir can be welcome. The gatekeeper is in the driver's seat though, and we may not be happy with many of his decisions. Fluctuating water levels are not helpful to either a trout-stream or its anglers. Since modest drainages are seldom dammed, small streams are generally more natural fisheries and easier to handicap.

Earlier I stated that the small stream is an ideal primer for the beginning reader. My reasons included

I've used up a good many minutes. Mediocre water usually produces in a mediocre way. Good, bad, or indifferent, the creek's arms, legs, fingers, and toes are built on a smaller frame. It's hard to get stuck on a bad sentence for very long!

Pocket water with trouty targets all around.

sharpness of detail plus the opportunity to see the print up close. A third aspect is just as important: the component parts of a small stream are necessarily restricted in size and closely spaced. This permits the angler to test all sorts of target water quickly. For example, we've been discussing shifting trout distribution during transitional phases of the season. When fishing a creek it's easy to flick your fly into shallow riffles, eddies, strong currents, and the deep center of pools all within a few minutes. Pieces of river anatomy are gross by comparison, so much so that I feel as if I were a Lilliputian wading over one of the giant Gulliver's parts. I get into a sort of Christmas morning syndrome. There's just too much to play with all around and all at once. I find myself surrounded by huge targets of less than the best quality and yet grading fair for potential. Instead of moving on, I'll pick away, casting here and there until

3
Stalking

BASICS

SURFACE TEXTURE

DEPTH

LOW PROFILE

FISH UPSTREAM

MOVE SLOWLY

SENTINELS

SPAWNING

STALKING HORSES

CAMOUFLAGE

FISHING OUT THE CAST

OVER-FISHING

UNDER-FISHING

WADING

Trout come from the factory with all manner of built-in warning devices. Although these are instinctive mechanisms, trout are superbly equipped to detect fraud. This is precisely what flyfishers find so intriguing. The trout's legendary wariness brings out the latent confidence man in us, the very desire to commit fraud. We would sell the poor fish the Brooklyn Bridge if we could, settling instead for the wooden nickels we call flies.

Caution is advisable in most fishing. When it comes to small streams, caution means stalking in the truest sense of the word. On big water there is the luxury of making long casts, whereas the brook-bound angler is wedged in right on top of his quarry. Forced up close and personal, we have no choice but to exercise the utmost care. Frankly, stalking is tedious, time-consuming, and difficult. The good news is that a stealthy, close aproach offers valuable benefits. To put it differently, there are definite liabilities involved in fishing at long range. Consider the following: (1) It is more difficult to place a fly on target from farther away. Small stream targets are themselves diminutive, and while throwing the line far enough is seldom an issue, accuracy and delicacy of presentation certainly are. There is an analogy to golf wherein the green is easier to hit and hold from 135 yards than from 185. This is true even for the best players regardless that the 135 yard effort is only 25 percent shorter. (2) Apart from hitting targets, creek casting lanes or avenues are frequently blocked by pro-

truding branches. The flying line has to get over, under, or between these obstructions in order to reach its destination. River targets are typically wide-open pieces of water. Shorter casts are far easier to control. (3) It is more difficult to follow a fly in or on the water from afar and to detect a rise or strike. The best possible visibility is critical. Beyond question, efficiency in setting the hook falls off at distance. (4) In presenting a fly via a natural drift, any degree of drag is undesirable. The longer the cast, the more line there will be on the water to be caught by currents that cause drag or an unnatural drift. At close range it's usually possible to lift much of the line free, thereby avoiding drag and obtaining a longer drift.

Enforced proximity, angler to trout, can make movement along the channel from one target area to the next hazardous. Rivers often provide a strip of beach or shoals for easy movement along the water's edge. Creek banks are seldom so accommodating, leaving one to splash pretty much through the middle of things. Major streams also tend to be hard-fished, and this leads to the establishment of bankside trails that never get worn in along less frequented creeks.

While stalking is an essential skill, it's necessary to keep things in perspective. The amount of stealth required varies with both time and place. Trout in a given stream and in a certain set of circumstances display a fairly uniform level of concern for their safety. This can range from extreme apprehension to a sort of fearless bravado. It follows that if the angler can identify the level of spookiness, he can adjust his tactics accordingly. As noted, the law of supply and demand is a very useful handle. The greater the availability of cover, the less important it will be to the trout and the less cautious they become. On this basis murky water has a calming, almost reassuring influence. By contrast, as summer water levels drop, portions of the stream that once offered cover are either high and dry or very shoal. The stream will also have cleared and slowed with much more smooth surface area. This scarcity of cover makes trout increasingly wary. However, the picture can suddenly change when there is a temporary glut of food and the trout are gorging themselves. In this circumstance they lose much of their natural caution. It's doubly fortunate when the runoff or a good rain brings both food and cover to a creek. Then the deck is really stacked in the fisherman's favor.

Are trout in hard-fished waters more suspicious than their cousins in more secluded streams? Fish that see a lot of artificials go by and have perhaps been hooked several times are clearly more selective about patterns and presentations. When it comes to spookiness though, I'm not sure it isn't the other way around. As a youth I foolishly developed a condescending attitude toward wilderness cutthroat, supposing them to be naive. In reality these fish are constantly on hair trigger. While perhaps open minded about checking out fly patterns, cutthroat are not otherwise easy to catch and will certainly not tolerate insults to their protective instincts. I'm convinced that the setting of a fishery has everything to do with spookiness. On angler-saturated streams trout appear to become accustomed to a constant parade. They seem to take the outlines of human torsos and flailing rods pretty much for granted. I remember feeling downright intimidated when I first visited famed Armstrong's Spring Creek near Livingston, Montana. Afraid that any casting mishap or tackle indiscretion would make me a laughing stock, I practically shook in my boots. I soon learned that when a hatch is on these most sophisticated of trout show much less concern for their safety than interest in filling their bellies. They'll take within spitting distance and not just on super-fine tippets either. I'll bet that the hypersensitivity

of wild trout in virginal fisheries is simply the other side of the coin. They are so accustomed to a near absence of angler sign that the smallest warning sets them off.

Getting a general feel for just how jumpy or brazen the trout are likely to be is important. Perhaps someday a mechanism will be invented for measuring trout "up-tightness" directly. I'll bet it would be an electronic device with a chromed case and a catchy name such as "Spook-O-Meter." They'd sell like hotcakes. However, until such instruments become available, common sense plus a little experience will go a long way.

Basics

Assuming that some level of stealth is in order, what's to be done? Let's begin with a basic principle: *Most of those features which provide cover for the trout also hide the fisherman from his quarry.* Stalking really amounts to turning the "cover" table on the fish. These shared cover features include roil, a choppy surface, and physical objects such as knuckles in the bank, streambed rocks, and so forth. It's a game of hide-and-go-seek, yet hardly a fair one from the trout's standpoint. Reflect that in order for the fish to know there's danger afoot they have to see or feel some evidence of an intruder's presence. By contrast, anglers don't necessarily need to see trout in order to catch them. We commonly fish a piece of water solely on the basis of its merit. When you think about it, the difference is really quite fundamental. To summarize, when cover is abundant we should take advantage of it. Bold approaches and short casts are both safe and sensible. When cover is scarce you've got to make the best out of what there is.

Surface Texture

I pay a lot of attention to the water's surface. As mentioned earlier, we think that in order for trout to see out clearly, the surface needs to be smooth. Fish certainly behave as if this were true. This form of angler cover doesn't have to be a spray-throwing chop either. Just some undulating bulges, as on the face of a current, do the job. The shallow riffle provides the toughest test of the rough-surface theory because trout in shoal water are supposed to be jittery anyway. Since it is possible to get quite close to fish in this kind of water without spooking them, there's something to the idea.

Depth

The question of depth brings up a contradiction. Going back to the "window," you'll remember the concept of a cone. The apex begins with the trout's eyes, and the base is an oval area in the surface film. Without resorting to geometry, it's apparent that the greater the height of the cone, the larger the diameter of the window. Therefore the deeper the trout, the more he sees of the outside world. This phenomenon should afford bottom-hugging fish outstanding protection. It ought to be just about impossible to get anywhere near fish in a deep pool without frightening them. In reality things don't necessarily work this way. Trout in pools just aren't that spooky. Although I'd not recommend charging right up to the very brink, neither is it necessary to cast from the next county. Maybe the trout can't see through a thick layer of water as well as we suppose. Possibly internal current swirls and variations blur images like a warped pane of glass. I've wondered too if fish feel so safe under a few feet of water that they aren't particularly vigilant. At any rate, just as trout give

deep water a good grade for cover, so can you—up to a point. And there's a matching corollary in contradictions: We'd expect fish lying in shallows to be safely approachable because their windows are small. Don't bet on it. When trout are lying under only a few inches of water they are likely to have their warning systems set on full amplitude and fine tuned. This is why a shallow, slick-surfaced glide, as at the tail of a pool, is the most difficult kind of water to stalk.

Low Profile

Let's take a more detailed look at this window business: A circular ring of "mirror" lies beyond the edges of the trout's window. Objects that might otherwise be seen through the ring are invisible because the surface film reflects the bottom. In cross section the mirror ring is wedge-shaped and thinnest where it leaves the water. In order for an angler to occupy the inner part of the ring without being seen he would almost have to lie flat. As he backs away into the thicker part of the wedge he might be able to squat, and farther back still, he could stand before his head and shoulders would enter the window area. It's a pleasingly simple formula but there's a hooker: Light rays bend as they pass through the surface film and this has the effect of greatly enlarging the window. Instead of continuing as a straight line, the edge of the window or "sill" gets bent sharply

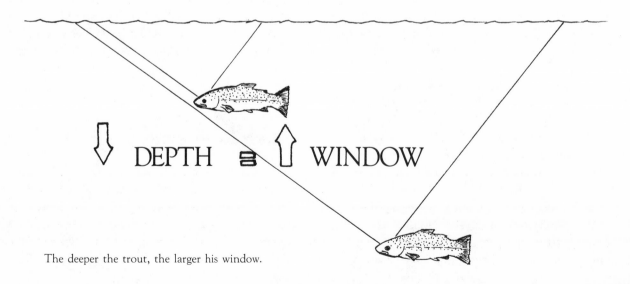

The deeper the trout, the larger his window.

Casting over the window ledge.

down toward the water surface. Indeed the angle at the window ledge is said to be only about 10 degrees. So according to principles of physics, the window view is something like that seen through a wide angle lens (or fisheye lens). That supposed 10-degree angle is awfully flat as you'll appreciate if you sit down with paper, pen-

WINDOW

The "bending" window sill makes things tough.

cil, and a protractor. These angles and lines depict a pretty discouraging situation. Depending on whether the fisherman is wading (so that less of him sticks up) or standing on an elevated bank, the closest he can come to the trout without entering the window area is somewhere between 25 and 40 feet. Diagram the trout deeper and things get worse. I didn't make up these

fishy physics. Diagrams of this sort replete with windows and mirrors have appeared in print for a long time.[2] I have no real quarrel with the window and ledge idea and I agree that staying low is a good plan. Hunkering down in one way or another allows the caster to cheat in the sense of getting closer to the target with safety than he could otherwise. This is an especially good ploy when working from an elevated bank. In flat-surfaced shallows I'll occasionally resort to a duck walk, casting from my haunches as long as creaking joints will permit. All this notwithstanding, I wouldn't take the window equation too mathematically. Real experiences astream suggest that certain liberties can be taken. There are ever so many times when according to calculation, the upper parts of me just about have to be in the window of a trout I'm pursuing. Yet I know the fish wasn't overly concerned when he takes my fly. Rather than his not caring, it's more likely that I either wasn't noticed or wasn't seen clearly. It's my suspicion that what the trout see out toward the horizons of the sills of their windows is blurred. Perhaps shapes are distorted and warped and forms run together as happens at the edges of an imperfect lens.

[2]Holland, Dan, *The Trout Fisherman's Bible* (Garden City, NY: Doubleday, 1949), p. 37.

Fish Upstream

There is one stalking technique that stands out above all others for fundamental simplicity and consistent utility. *Fish upstream!* Trout holding in current face upstream themselves. According to biologists the window cone is functionally tilted forward, thus increasing straight-ahead vision while leaving the trout with a blind spot toward the rear. If this is so an approach from behind ought to be safest. It works. I've been amazed at how close I can get to trout so long as I stay directly behind them. A stealthy, backside stalk can put you into cozy casting position, almost breathing down their necks. Of course there's nothing to be gained by absolutely refusing to fish downstream as if some grand principle were being violated. Sometimes a good piece of water will be shielded from below by physical obstructions. Or currents can preclude more than a split second's worth of drift. If targets like this can be worked from above, why not? On larger streams downstream drifts to selective fish are effective when a particular riser is to be tempted. The tactic is to show the fly to the fish before the leader comes along. However, these are individual, targeted trout in a setting that's vastly different from a brushy creek. Generally speaking, you'll frighten far fewer trout by fishing upstream. Achieving a natural drift will be much easier too.

Move Slowly

The idea that sudden movements are likely to frighten wild things certainly applies to trout. "Slow and smooth" are good adjectives for the small stream angler to live by. I believe that when your image enters the fringe of a fish's window, movement will often determine whether or not you'll be apprehended. It's the fast, jerky actions that seem to trigger the alarm. The example that best demonstrates this is the pool in a narrow, steeply climbing canyon. Wading up the channel's staircase you spot a tiny pool up ahead, spilling over a little falls. In order to work the target you'll have to see how it is laid out, where the currents are, and where brush threatens along the banks. So slowly, slow-

ly you insinuate your head into the little pool's window. (This is an acceptable form of window-peeking.) To your delight the several occupants have not detected your presence. The trout continue to laze about unsuspectingly. Your pulse quickens as line is carefully stripped from the reel for one short cast. The leader is checked for loops and snags. The time has come, and with a forward flip of the rod your fly flutters onto the pool's surface as gently as a falling leaf. A beautiful sequence—except the split second the rod moves to propel the cast the trout scatter as if pursued by the very demons of hell! This has happened to me so many times that the whole scenario is all too familiar. There's no doubt that this single, necessarily brisk movement of the rod is responsible. No matter that the flyrod is but a slender stick that might pass for a branch blowing in the breeze, that sudden movement is recognized as unnatural. Regardless of whether there's a target close at hand, I've found it wise to make most movements in controlled and leisurely fashion, even the wiping of a nose. The angler who adopts the habit of sidling along casually in the process of progressing to a fresh casting position is invariably better off. This precludes boorish practices such as splashy striding, acrobatic rock hopping, or bush trampling in the manner of a foraging hippopotamus. Intent on the creek up ahead, it's easy enough to trip over a piece of driftwood or slip on a mossy rock. On this account I prefer a shuffling mode of locomotion wherein I lift my feet only enough to clear objects in my path. I'm sure I appear to be either inebriated or terribly tired, but while wading I kick up a lot less debris and send out fewer waves that may spread alarm. When fishing from soggy banks in a pasture or marshy meadow, the springy soil is very apt to transmit vibrations into the water for some distance. Here too I've found it helpful to slide my feet along rather than picking them up as a normal person would.

Sentinels

One of the frustrations that small stream anglers must endure is the "sentinel phenomenon." Sentinels are trout that get frightened by a fisherman's movements. The frustration comes when these fish flee helter-skelter into the midst of target water ahead, spoiling it. I don't imply that the frenzied arrival of sentinels merely detracts somewhat from the angler's chances. I mean they are flat-out ruined! It's all over. Sentinels often are tiny fish that occupy unimpressive pockets along the banks, water that is passed by purposely. This is a large part of the problem. These pesky minnows frequent such trifling pockets that it's hard to know just where they'll be, and this makes them hard to avoid. There is no guaranteed method for dealing with these fright-mongers. By working upstream there's always the hope of slipping by them. If you suspect that one or several of the little tattletales lies against the far bank this is a good ploy. Even if they do flee when you're across from them, they may scatter downstream rather than up.

Long pools with thin glides at the tails are especially difficult. Glides are very likely to hold sentinels and thus serve to protect the entire pool. Trying to inch up within range of the really pretty water without scattering the sentinels can drive you crazy. Each is a potential arrow of fear aimed at the heart of the target. The only solution I know is to climb clear out of the creek and back from the water. Then, if you're lucky, it may be possible to get opposite the pool's head, standing on the bank and casting from that vantage. It's a side-saddle approach. On occasion it's necessary to fish this way through much of the day. Last September I took on the shrunken remains of what had been a fair-sized brook back in June. I realized that I would have to contend with a triad of additive difficulties, including thin, clear water, densely packed alders overhanging both banks, and sentinels at every station. This combination turned out to be even worse than feared. The trout were delighted to come up for my grasshopper imitation, no problem there, but getting the fly to them without first activating the sentinel system was a near impossibility. Earlier in the year this creek had lots of fish-filled flat water. Now those flats were but inches deep with the trout concentrated in pools, most of them guarded by a glide. When I made long casts from a safe distance I commonly caught the tip of a branch. Or the line, falling on the quiet water, would spread panic "up-creek" in a hurry. I finally quit wading altogether. Instead I'd find a likely pool well up ahead and identify a marker of some sort on the bank opposite its head.

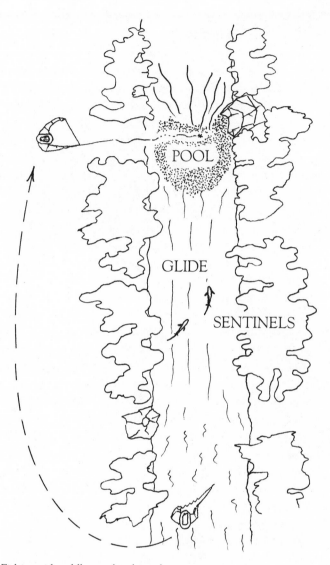

Fishing sidesaddle can be the only way to go.

The banks were steep, overgrown, and prickly, but I patiently bushwhacked until I drew parallel to the target, hoping to find enough of a break in the alders to cast through. Lobbing the line downhill and sidesaddle, I had just one shot. I had to hit the gap on the first cast, and the throw could neither be short nor long since it was seldom possible to pick up for another try without snagging. The way things went I had about a 50-50 chance of finding a gap and about the same chance of pulling off the cast. Therefore, three out of four bramble-busting expeditions were for naught. When I did get the fly to its destination though, I invariably rose and usually hooked a fish. Further, these were fat brownies and rainbows up to 14 inches. Can you imagine the fracas that's involved in getting fish like this landed in such a setting? At the day's end I had released 18 trout, I was scratched, tired—and happy!

Spawning

I have mixed feelings about fishing during active spawning. On the one hand you may encounter large trout running out of lakes or rivers into feeder streams. On the other hand, it makes simple sense to leave the fish alone during this period. In any case, I have run into spawning brown trout on a number of occasions in the late fall, and it is an interesting phenomenon. They will be queued in special and rather unusual sorts of water such as the very tails of runs where the water thins to a few inches and picks up speed. Riffles with swift flow and similar depth are another site. Early in the spawning process these fish are very active, and while preoccupied, they are also on hair trigger. These spawners are exceptionally easy to spook and become deadly sentinels. Even the fish massed out in the riffles will flee at the slightest provocation. These trout may attack a fly, but their attention is directed toward more primal matters. I've found that it's best to skirt the tails and riffles altogether, concentrating instead on the upper portions of current systems where the flow dumps into the deep gut of the run or pool. It seems that those fish that are not engaged in procreation are most likely to be found in this sort of water.

Before we leave the subject, sentinels with fur and feathers have also plagued me from time to time. A mother merganser with her brood of little water runners, lined up like boxcars behind the locomotive, is quite capable of spooking a stream for hours. She'll stay just far enough ahead to keep things stirred up, and should you try to pass, mom merganser and her kids just shove it to the floorboard. I've had mallards do the same thing, although they're usually considerate enough to fly some distance, leaving you a little water in between. And feebleminded cows can give you fits. I re-

member one hysterical heifer in particular: Three of us had it in mind to work through the length of a long meadow. Since the trail hit the meadow at its upper end, we began to walk toward the bottom, intending to fish back. This adolescent cow was browsing contentedly along the edge of an undercut bank as we passed. Surely we meant her no harm, yet she must have perceived us as creatures of evil intention, for she leapt headlong into the stream. The water happened to be deep, and we laughed as the panicked heifer swam frantically for safety. It was even funnier when the bungling bovine attempted to scale the opposite bank, caving in several cubic yards of black soil in the process. It wasn't so funny, though, when roil released from the crumbled bank just about ruined our fishing! Then there was the pair of friendly pups I met near Aspen. One was a Lab, the other a red setter and both were overflowing with the joy of each other's company on this summer day. When I ventured along, their happiness knew no bounds. How could I ignore such playful comrades dashing from bank to bank, hither and yon? It would have been hard for they both took great delight in chasing down my floating fly. Once I didn't rip the fly off the water quickly enough and the Lab nailed it in mid-air. Fortunately he was just lip hooked and only superficially. It was fun to tell about at dinner although I wasn't as cordial as I might have been the next afternoon when my friends rushed down the trail to meet me, tails wagging.

Stalking Horses

Apart from avoiding sentinels there's another very practical means for making safe, close approaches to reach a casting position. It's a technique that takes the so-called window right out of the picture and without requiring you to pretend that you're only three feet tall. Simply, this involves getting some physical object between you and the trout. The object might be a boulder, a deadfall tree limb, a bend in the bank, or a clump of brush. All serve nicely if it's possible to line up the cover object between yourself and the quarry. This stalking-horse technique often affords point blank approaches to fish that would otherwise flee in terror. But if the trout is hidden on the far or blind side of the stalking-horse object, how to know when to set the hook? This is part of the chicanery of creekcraft that I enjoy the most. Many times you will hear a telltale splash that signals a take. You should also watch the end of the line or leader butt where it drapes across the back of the stalking-horse for a sudden twitch. It's also possible to calculate the point in time following your cast when the fly should have reached the heart of the target area. Then gently lift your rod enough to tighten the line. An explosion may erupt on the far side of the stalking horse! Fishing blind is an enormously satisfying way to finagle fish when they are irritatingly flighty and cover is scanty.

The best stalking-horse setting of all is a meandering meadow stream with some depth. Tight knuckles in the bank make marvelous shields. You just wade up close to one side of the knuckle, profile low, and lob your fly across.

Bank knuckles make ideal stalking-horses.

I've not found that camouflage clothing or face paint are necessary for successful small stream stalking. I'd merely avoid light or bright colors in favor of neutral shades. Utilization of natural cover combined with cautious movement is far more important than one's attire.

Fishing Out the Cast

Fishing-out-the-cast is an excellent habit I learned many years ago from Ray Bergman's classic *Trout*.[3] Fishing-out is a dependable yardstick for measuring both the degree of spookiness exhibited by the trout and the effectiveness of your stalking tactics. Fishing-out the cast really amounts to seeing what happens to a fly that is *closer* to you than your major target, that is between you and the area of prime interest. By definition, fishing-out water is somewhat second rate. It might read as only mediocre, or you might have already made a cast or two into that part of the stream. Most commonly this is water that seems too close for comfort. Fishing-out applies to any kind of cast or method of presentation. It might mean watching a naturally drifting fly float back almost to your feet, or it might mean pulling a retrieved fly back to within rod's length. The point is that if a strike is forthcoming in this inferior water, the observation is noteworthy. It tells you several things. You know that, on this occasion at least, your approach toward the primary target didn't spook the water closer in. Also, by inference, you can't have spoiled the target that lay beyond. Not only is this reassuring, it also suggests that you may be able to get away with more aggressive stalks and shorter casts when targets of like nature come along later. On the contrary, if the close-in water persistently fails to produce, you are possibly sending sentinels on their deadly missions. It's all too easy to overlook sentinels that have done their damage while concentrating on targets farther upstream. Fishing-out the cast is not a natural thing for most of us, myself included. Once the fly has gotten through the primary target, it's automatic to lose enthusiasm for that particular presentation. We want to get on to the next one and to sample new water where the grass looks greener. Be that as it may, fishing-out is almost always a good idea. You derive valuable information that will

[3]Ray Bergman, *Trout* (New York: Alfred A. Knopf, 1964), pp. 16–17.

help to tune your Stalk-O-Meter while catching at least a few fish in the bargain. Besides, fishing-out doesn't take much extra time.

There is another fishing-out ploy that's based on mishap: Imagine that you have just started to work a promising piece of water when the fly gets hung up on the streambed well out toward the target and can't be twitched free. Rather than giving up, wade slowly to the snag, keeping low, and release the fly as stealthily as possible. Then continue to cast to the target. Once in awhile a trout will take, regardless that you are "too close." When this happens you have learned something and hooked a fish too. What's there to lose?

Over-Fishing

While fishing-out is a good practice, it is also possible to overwork a small stream. An angler faces a continuous series of choices concerning which targets he will go after and which will be bypassed. This never-ending process of decision making is one of the most entertaining aspects of creekcraft. Two extremes of attitude are possible. The fisherman might decide to work only the very best pieces of water. Alternatively he could tackle every target in sight. The attitude a fisherman adopts will determine how much stream he'll cover during the day. Working petty pieces of water greatly slows progress. Further, in the process of casting to minor targets you sometimes ruin better ones. In this regard I often think of Sancho Panza, Don Quixote's faithful companion. Literature's classic pragmatist, Sancho preferred to keep his eye on the "main chance" rather than flirting with ventures of uncertain outcome. There's not much question as to how Sancho would conduct himself along a small trout stream. He'd concentrate on the best bets, forgetting the rest. Sancho wasn't dumb, and he'd know all about sentinels and that the more minor targets you address, the more fright-mongers you'll send scurrying. Just wading a few steps to get into position to cast might prove fatal: a dragging fly will trigger them as will your shadow or the line falling across their lies. And even experts get hung up attempting to hit occluded targets. If the secondary piece of water lies adjacent to a really good piece of water, as yet unfished, it's

likely that both will be ruined in the process of getting free. So as with sentinels, fooling around with potential entanglements is hazardous. This is why going for the throat, first thing, can pay off. In football it has been said that when the ball is put into the air three things can happen and of these, two are bad. Similarly, when a fly is cast the provisional outcomes include two negatives, spooking the trout or getting snagged versus one positive, i.e., completing the cast as planned. Thus I constantly admonish myself to avoid frivolous or unnecessary casts. Have a reason and a plan every time you launch your fly.

Under-Fishing

But don't get me wrong, target elitism isn't always the best policy. In a sense it's contrary to fishing-out. When there's ample cover and the trout are spread out and eager, it's far more fun to shop around. Taking on those intermediate and even low-value pieces of water can't help but hone reading skills, and attempting tough casts is excellent practice. When the fish are willing to take in water of all sorts there's a lot to be learned. Those days are precious. Just keep in mind that it is possible to ruin the best water by picking too compulsively at its skirts. Fortunately it's not a matter of committing to one attitude over the other. We can work out our salvation for the day through observation, trial and error, and common sense. We can and should try it both ways: Sancho's, the fish-it-all approach, and in-between as well.

In the final analysis anglers are always seeking a happy medium. It all boils down to the question: "What proportion of targets am I willing to spoil in return for improved casting efficiency, control of drag, and ease in setting the hook?" Getting the answer right for the conditions at hand will greatly improve an angler's success. I personally believe the answer should *not* be: "I'll take whatever measures are necessary to avoid spoiling any water." Now if the issue involved running red lights or passing on curves I'd agree with the safety first policy. But pieces of fish-containing water are usually liberally scattered along stream channels. There are plenty more where the failed ones came from. Still the "Damn the Torpedoes" philosophy isn't necessarily best either. So much depends on getting your "Stalk-O-Stat" set properly.

Wading

If you are serious about fishing any stream, you must wade. I think it's plain dumb to try to fish dryshod. Not getting your feet wet is like going out for football hoping to keep your uniform clean. Besides, creek banks are usually so brushy you'll have to wade. What if the banks are open and grassy and the channel is narrow? No matter, you'll still want to ford and reford. Most pieces of water can be worked better from one bank than the other. One casting position almost always offers some advantage, and this holds for rills no more than a couple of feet across. Bank position is only part of the story. Casting from the creekbed proper is useful in avoiding obstructions, lessening problems with drag, making the best use of cover, and keeping a low profile. If fishing a stream well as opposed to half-heartedly matters, why accept the crippling handicap that keeping your feet dry imposes? Wading and getting wet don't have to be the same thing of course, but for me boots are a bother unless the alternative is frostbite or hypothermic shock. I prefer to fish wet in a pair of wading shoes. This is a Philistine's approach, and you won't catch many sophisticates clad in tennies. However it's seldom that a creekfisher gets wet above the knees, and moist pant legs are welcome on a warm day. It's also noteworthy that rubber-ripping encounters with barbed wire, jagged limbs, and thorny branches are a good deal more likely along overgrown banks of small streams than on well-worn river trails. Not everyone agrees. I've seen anglers encased in chest-high waders laboring along a brushy brook like elephantine caddis.

Whatever your choice, I strongly recommend some form of fabric sole. The size of a stream doesn't matter when it comes to falling. The tiniest rivulet is capable of growing slime that's just as treacherous as any river's. While drowning may not be an issue, the potential consequences of a pratfall are.

After all this talk about stealth I should acknowledge that there is also an anti-stalking school. The following experience was described to me by a friend from Missouri: Walter was fishing Montauk State Park one day when he came upon a lady sitting by the stream, pole in hand. As he drew closer she put her rig down and struggled to pick up a head-sized rock. Staggering to the bank, she chucked it in, Ker-plosh! Bemused, my friend couldn't resist asking her how things were going. "They've been napping all afternoon," she replied. "But I just woke 'em up." There are times when I'm tempted to do the same.

4

Special Casts for Small Water

THE "OTHER HAND"

CLEAR THE DECKS

WATCH THE TROUBLE

GET THE *FIRST* CAST IN

DON'T OVER-FISH

I once watched Lefty Kreh, the famed flycaster, work his magic on the Henry's Fork. He had almost the entire line rocketing back and forth. His loop was so tight that the line's path became a blurred streak of concentrated energy. Every flyfisher aspires to the ability to throw long and rifle straight. Intuitively, that's what casting should be all about. Most of us worship at the shrine of long-distance methods such as the intercontinental double haul. This kind of talent is largely wasted on small streams. Creek casts of necessity tend toward the short and crooked. Although it might seem that abbreviated casts should be relatively easy, they're not. Tight-quarters casting involves a variety of tricky techniques, some of them unorthodox. The emphasis is on touch and finesse rather than upon high line speed and tight loops. It's a different kind of skill. In view of the physical restrictions with which the creek caster must deal, it's not surprising that novel ways and means of propelling line, leader, and fly have evolved. I classify them as follows:

The Roll Cast
Sidearm Casts
The Steeple Cast
Slack-line Casts
"Non-casts" (explanation to follow)

The Roll Cast: As a kid did you move the lawn sprinkler by rolling a loop of hose out toward the sprinkler head? By giving the segment of hose a sideways twist you could position the sprinkler without getting wet. It was less trouble and more fun than turning the water off and moving the thing by hand. The roll cast is based on the identical principle. An angler preparing for a roll cast lifts the rod toward the vertical. The rod is tilted back slightly, pointing a little away from his torso. This could be called "loading" the cast since the "ammunition" for the roll is the length of line lifted off the water. A brisk forward snap of wrist and forearm then fires the lifted line in the form of a loop in the precise plane directed by the rod's path. The rolling loop moves progressively along the length of the line, reaches the end, and incorporates the leader momentarily. Eventually the leader loop opens when the fly comes along, and the energy within the cast is dissipated as the fly is deposited on the water. The whole thing is beautifully simple and free of opportunity for error. It's truly hard to screw up a roll cast. It has always surprised me that experts who write about flycasting pay so little attention to this method. I suspect it's too easy a thing for them; beneath their dignity. Most of those sophisticated technical terms and concepts having to do with open and closed loops, tailing loops, line speed and wobble, etc., hardly apply to the apple pie roll cast. Reading "how to" books and articles about flycasting can be scary. There are so many things to worry about. I'm rather attracted to a mechanism that places the fly where I want it without raising the question of how many errors I'm committing in the process.

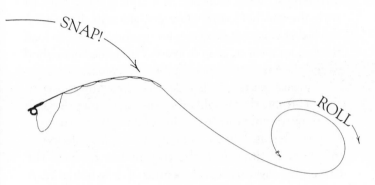

The roll cast snaps the fly forward crisply and with precision.

The roll cast is loaded with helpful features. First and foremost, there's no backcast. In brushy surroundings this can mean the difference between getting the fly to its destination and becoming enmeshed in the green stuff behind. Because of the absence of a backcast, the roll is excellent for wind, and it won't tire your arm through the longest day. The roll cast is also a quick, accurate, and safe way of presenting a weighted fly. The standard overhead cast with weight on the end of the leader is cumbersome, and you can drive the hook into the back of your neck or ear. Although a roll cast can punch out 40 feet of line, when the distance to be covered is short there's no need to load up with a lot of line and rod lift. Just hold the rod in front and a little to one side with only slight arm elevation. It's enough ammunition for a cast of 25 feet or so, and since the rolling loop faithfully follows the plane of the forward snapping rod, accuracy is outstanding. It's almost like aiming down a gun barrel. A roll cast can be pretty much premeasured for length too. The rolling loop is going to reach just as far as the length of line and leader you have out beyond the rod tip. A yard or so of extra extension will be added by the rod itself since the rod ends up pointed toward the target.

I'm reminded of pegging a dart toward the bull's-eye of a target—a minimum of motion plus precision control. While I often use the roll when fishing a weighted fly, it's also a very handy means of propelling dry flies. When the rolling loop picks up the fly it leaps off the surface cleanly at a sharp angle. This crisp take-off shakes loose droplets of water, partially drying the fly.

Sidearm Casts are made with the rod more or less parallel to the water. These casts are very useful on small

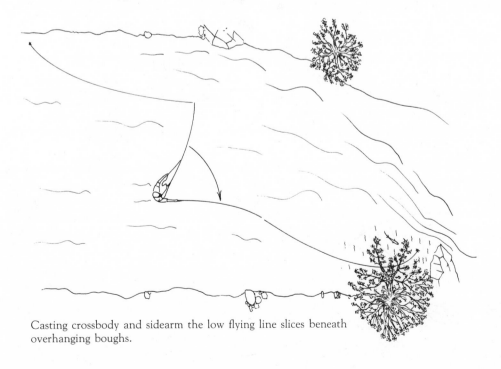

Casting crossbody and sidearm the low flying line slices beneath overhanging boughs.

water despite the fact that a flat rod sweep takes up more lateral space along a narrow channel than a vertical sweep. Sidearm casts keep the line low so that it fits under obstructions in front or behind. And rather than wasting space, sidearm casts make the best use of what is available, meanwhile avoiding hangups. Facing upstream a right-handed caster may throw sidearm when on or close to the left bank. This places the rod and flying line out over the open stream channel. When hard by the right bank he can employ a cross body cast. Facing quartering and upstream, he holds the rod across his chest during the casting stroke with the back of his hand facing the target. This again shifts the rod and line away from the bank and into open space over the water. Sidearm presentations are not as inherently accurate as casts with the rod held vertical. The fly may land either to the left or right of target and line speed has to be kept above stalling since it is low to the ground or water. These casts seem awkward at first, but the mechanics are simple, and accuracy improves quickly with practice.

It isn't always necessary to hold the rod absolutely flat to the surface. A three-quarters position of about 45 degrees between vertical and horizontal will often keep the line low enough and is more comfortable. One of the most useful techniques of all is a short roll cast with the rod held three-quarters, sidearm. Even with the rod at this angle you can lift up enough line to load the cast for a short, crisp delivery. This remedial method of fly placement is super for brushy creeks.

Sidearm casts are also ideal for throwing curves to cheat currents that would otherwise cause drag. A curve is an upstream-pointing belly of line that crosses a tongue of swift flow with the fly on the far side. Since the fly can't drag until the current has reversed the curve, this cast buys extra seconds of drag-free drift. A curve that leaves the fly to the right and below the belly is thrown sidearm by lobbing the line lazily on the forward cast. This sluggish delivery fails to straighten the line, leaving the leader and fly behind. The same "tired" delivery off a cross body cast creates a left-sided curve. These are touch casts. The placement of the fly

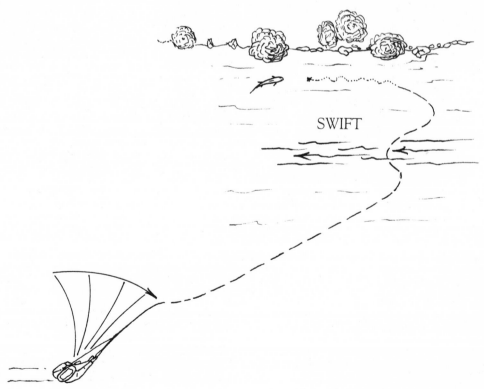

SWIFT

A crossbody curve cast cheats drag.

and the depth of the bend in the curve depend upon rod angle plus the amount of drive in its forward movement. Curves are really quite simple at close range once you get the hang.

The Steeple Cast is just a variation of the normal overhead cast. It is designed to throw the back cast as high as possible to clear rearward obstructions. The steeple hopes to accomplish the same thing as the sidearm methods by going over rather than under. The familiar clock-face diagram depicts rod position at various points in the casting sequence. The angler faces 9 o'clock such that in the process of false casting the rod passes back and forth between about 10:30 and 1 o'clock. In throwing a cast the rod might reach back to 2 o'clock, sweeping forward to about 9:30 as the line falls onto the water. In steeple casting the plane of rod sweep gets tilted into an arc that's higher behind and lower in front than normal. Thus the rear sweep of the rod on the back cast is arrested somewhat prematurely, as at 12:30. In addition the rod arm is extended by straightening the elbow. The wrist too is semi-locked, meaning that much of the joint movement in steepling is taken over by the shoulder. This kicks the line almost straight up at the top of the cast. The steeple is not entirely graceful and has a stiff, awkward look to it. Further, there is danger of slapping the water in front with your fly due to the forward tilt of the casting arc. Steepling is not difficult though and will save you all sorts of trips to the trees.

Even when you are not making full-fledged steeple casts it's healthy for the creek fisherman to keep all of his back casts reasonably high unless there is reason to do otherwise. A high line usually avoids more difficulty than it finds. Employ a slightly straightened elbow, a wrist that is other than floppy, and somewhat "early" rod position at the top of the back cast. Too much wrist or elbow flex lead to late rod positions on the back cast such as 2:30 or 3 o'clock, and this causes the fly and leader to spank the water or ground behind. You can get away with this on a lake or river. Try it on small water, though, and I'll promise that your drooping terminal tackle will go out of its way to get into trouble. These minor modifications, the firm wrist and elbow, and noontime rod position amount to a slight modulation of the standard cast. They merely convey a steeple

flavor or theme to the finished product. The high back cast plays an ongoing and vital role in saving your time, your flies, and your temper.

Slackline Casts are means of dealing with drag, but unlike curve casts they are not focused upon a specific problem current. Drag is a special nuisance in fishing a bounding brook because of a diversity of close-set, minor currents of varying direction and speed. These wisps and threads of flow catch, twist, and generally torture the terminal tackle. They cause flies to behave in ways that are strange and unnatural. There is no short-term solution to the threat of drag so dependable as a slackline cast. The principle is the same as in curve casts except that instead of forming one big bend, the end of the line and leader come down in a series of little bends, squiggles, and wiggles. Before miscreant currents can cause the fly to drag they will have to iron out every last curlicue. This is why throwing a ruler-straight line across complex currents is not as desirable as "casting crooked." Slackline casting is dependent upon line velocity, more particularly *falling* velocity during the forward cast. A flyline can be likened to a projectile that is thrown by the rod. Unfolding line necessarily has a certain amount of weight and variable momentum as befits its capacity as a projectile. Now if that velocity is insufficient to carry the line and leader out in a straight path as the cast is completed, they will fall akimbo onto the surface—like the proverbial wounded duck. There are several ways to put some shimmy into the end of a cast. The most primitive is to make an overhead cast with a feeble forward rod motion. Just as in throwing a right curve, if the forward cast is sluggish the line will describe a big, open loop. It will also run out of momentum and stall in midair before it gets straightened out. To further increase this out-of-gas forward flight you can let go of the line held in your left or non-rod hand as the rod comes forward, just as in shooting line for a long throw. Slack from between the stripping guide and reel gets pulled out by the forward flying line. This will further dampen the momentum of the line and add more complexity to the squiggle. The "uphill cast" is another way of looking at the same idea. Pretend that the fly is being lobbed onto the surface of an imaginary platform elevated some 15 feet above the surface. Casting onto this high platform, the rod tip stops at 11 o'clock rather than at the usual 9:30 position. The line and leader may straighten, but they will be pointing upwards at an angle when the energy of the cast is exhausted. As a result, they fall to the surface in a series of irregular pleats, again the wounded duck analogy.

The parachute cast was first described by the late Charles Ritz.[4] It's an overhead cast of the ordinary sort with the arm held way high, above shoulder level. Unlike the steeple cast, the arc is normal. Once the forward cast has come to its completion, more or less straightened out but still in midair, the angler quickly drops his arm and hand to belt level, as if suddenly paralyzed. This too causes the line and leader to flutter down ever so gently. If the forward part of the parachute presentation is feeble, the line and leader will develop undulations as they fall.

Another method that requires some tight timing is the terminal rod jerk. Here you pull back on the rod tip just as the forward cast straightens. It's like pulling the line up short by its collar. For me, this is the least controllable of the slackline techniques.

It is evident that all sorts of combinations are possible. Wind can have a great deal of impact on slacklining, either pro or con. If Nature gave fisherfolk a say as to how, when, and in which direction the wind would blow I imagine most of us would opt for a stiff breeze from behind. That's the way to get long, straight casts. Not us small stream types. We'd lobby in favor of a gentle breeze, head on! As long as the blow doesn't reach gale proportions, wind in the face creates gorgeous slack. Turn things around 180 degrees and the slackliner is in trouble, for his most carefully planned and executed wrinkles are going to get ironed out. Wind from the side is killing too. Because of low terminal velocity the line gets pushed and bullied all over the place by cross breezes. Regardless, slacklining is a staple in the repertoire of the creek caster. Throwing at least a little slack can become a habit, even as the high backcast. Slack is such good, cheap insurance against both subtle and more obvious drag. I like to think of slackline casting in baseball terms. I draw an analogy to throwing "junk," or slow stuff, and it's not a bad one. Like the pitcher who has lost his blazing fastball and smoking slider, you can get a lot of fish out with these change of pace and

knuckleball casts on small, swift streams. Like off-speed pitches, slackline casts require more finesse than muscle.

Many times you will be able to find a flat-surfaced rock, knuckle in the bank, or dry gravel bar that can be used as a platform to hold the end of the line or leader butt above the water. By positioning yourself so that the platform is directly in line with the target, the terminal tackle can be drape-cast over the object where it is protected from the pull of passing currents. This is particularly useful when you can't stand close enough to lift the line and rearward leader from the surface with your rod for fear of frightening the quarry. This tactic may seem too obvious for comment, yet I sometimes forget to look for such opportunities. If is only after my fly has dragged that I see how I could have used a platform to make the presentation more easily and safely. These platforms are really stalking horses of a different kind that give the small stream angler an edge in dealing with drag.

Non-casts are means of getting a fly into the vicinity of a trout without making a normal cast. Non-casts utilize mechanisms which are at best ungainly and, at worst, uncouth. These are mechanisms devoid of orthodoxy and politesse. But ask yourself, if you could catch fish *only* by resorting to non-casts, wouldn't you? Non-casting is something one turns to when there is no other way. The setting is most often a narrow brook, bound up in baleful brush where even a roll cast is impossible. Nonetheless, given the availability of adequate cover, it's possible to prosper within the limits of your very shadow! Non-casts are really just ways to get the fly and trout together with an absolute minimum of rod movement. The bow-and-arrow cast is a stunt I first watched a spinfisher perform at an exhibition. He sprung the rod deeply, bow-like, by pulling back on the lure with his hand, meanwhile pinching the monofilament tight against the rod barrel with a finger of his right hand. Releasing the lure just a split second before the monofilament, he could hit a teacup at 30 feet. You can copy this method of lure propulsion with a fly rig too, although the heavier line won't shoot to any extent. A big, weighted nymph may have enough moxie to pull out a little line, but practically, the cast won't go much further beyond the rod tip than the rod's length plus a couple of extra feet. With the rod held flat this can

---

[4]Charles Ritz, *A Flyfisher's Life* (New York: Henry Holt & Co., 1959), p. 137.

Draped across a grassy bank, the line escapes a current that would have quickly dragged the fly.

still be enough to reach a secluded target beneath an overhanging bough. The bow-and-arrow is probably the only cast that is more easily made with spinning gear.

It is an elegant cast compared with the primitive "pendulum swing." Armed with a long branch, a length of vine, and a bone hook, Neanderthal man probably swung his bait out underhand, no clock face nonsense. Nor am I too proud to regress to this evolutionary stage. I'll readily accept throwback status if I have to. You can also put just a little wrist snap into the swing. It's really an underhand roll cast with just enough force to carry out a few extra feet of line. Say that you're standing on the downstream side of a tree trunk that bridges a brook with deep water on the far side. What better way to ease the leader over the hurdle and into the target? You can also flick the old wrist to the right or left, holding the rod parallel to the surface for ingenious if abbreviated sidearm (sidewrist) presentations. This too takes some touch and familiarity with the amount of spring in the rod's tip, but accuracy is high and there's little danger of snags with these swings, flips, and flicks.

Under exceptionally trying circumstances I've reached the very depths of depravity by throwing, yes, throwing the fly with my left hand. It almost has to be

a weighted fly or leader with split shot, but you can propel an artificial some 20 feet this way so long as there's ample slack. I'll only resort to this final humiliation in the tightest spots where I feel that any rod movement would get me snagged. But throwing may not be the ultimate disgrace; there's "fly pushing." Assume that you are wading up the center of a murky creek in a segment where the best water is along the bank beneath a fringe of willow sweepers trailing in the current. You hold the rod at arm's length, angled toward the bank and flat to the surface. With a rod of reasonable length and a very short leader, say 4 feet, you can literally push the fly ahead of your slowly advancing thigh and 6 or 7 feet to one side. Given enough current to carry away wading ripples, it's surprising what can happen. I had all kinds of fly-pushing excitement last June on a brook that was still high and discolored by the runoff. Its bed was mostly clay and sand with undercut banks, and I noticed an occasional crayfish sculling for cover. I eventually caught a fat brownie with several crawdads in its gaster. Talk about a tight belt! The lobster-like carcasses were nearly 2 inches long, stretching the trout's stomach to near-bursting. Glutted though they must have been, those brownies literally charged a thick-bodied streamer when I pushed the fly ahead with a pulsing motion.

We've discussed certain casts that have special roles in small stream fishing. The *false cast*, however, is potentially negative. False casting partially air dries a fly and also roughly pre-measures a cast for distance and aim. For some anglers false casting is a soothing, calming exercise. Unfortunately, it can become a sort of nervous tic, a ritualistic preamble to the real thing. I'd cut down on false casting as much as possible for several reasons. As noted earlier, while branches blow in the breeze, they do not beat rhythmically back and forth like a flyrod. The trout clearly notice this difference. Second, the more you throw a fly around on brushy streams, the more accidents you're going to have. It's inevitable. You can hand dry a fly very nicely by blotting it, preening back its hackles, and adding more floatant if needed. There's no need to whip it about. (For blotting I carry a strip of absorbent cloth pinned to the inside of my vest's lapel. It's out of my way, yet handy for squeezing the wet out of a fly.) As to testing for length and accuracy before making the definitive cast, you may have to do without.

The "Other Hand"

It's all too easy to forget that the non-rod hand is a busy and essential partner. This is just as true for small water as large. In addition to controlling slack, adjusting line length, and releasing line for shooting, your free hand can accelerate line speed. Whenever the length of the line in motion and airborne is *shortened*, the velocity of the flying line will increase. When your left hand (assuming that most of us are right-handed) pulls in even a little line, say 6 inches worth, line speed will kick up. This manipulation can be put to good use in a number of ways. If you see that the cast is a bit weak and is going to land to one side of its intended destination, a left hand tug will move the terminal tackle over just where you wanted it. Similarly, if you suspect that the cast is going to fall short, as when a breeze erupts, a gentle tromp on the accelerator via a left-hand strip should provide the extra drive needed to make up the gap.

When fishing a wet fly upstream, natural drift, you'll want to watch the leader as it drifts back for telltale signs of a take. In this particular circumstance too much slack will damp out twitches that signal a strike, whereas a reasonably straight leader telegraphs this information much more quickly. One of the best ways to straighten a leader is through a left-hand pull just before the forward cast falls to the surface. This works nicely with any cast including the roll. You can also throw a shallow left curve toward the opposite bank by casting sidearm from the right side. If you strip in line sharply at the same time the rod snaps forward to deliver the cast, the leader and end of the line duck low and dive to the left, skimming the surface. It's a nifty means of getting a fly under a canopy of boughs and into holding water hard up against the bank while the curve temporarily foils a tongue of current.

The left hand can also slow line speed when you sense that the throw is a little too long or strong. It's just a matter of letting go so that a little slack slides out to sap the forward drive of the line, a "mini-shoot." When I consciously keep track of my left hand and what it's up to, I find that it fiddles around all the time. I'll catch it releasing a little slack here, tugging in a few inches there, and generally fine tuning my casts. I appreciate what my south paw does for me.

No matter how experienced, the creek caster frequently finds himself between Scylla and Charybdis. In fancy terms this means caught between a cliff and a whirlpool or between a rock and a hard place. Along small streams cliffs are a reality, whereas the maelstrom might be a shallow pool filled with spooky trout, the whole enclosed by a green tapestry of trouble. In the interest of maximizing successes and minimizing frustrations, I try to follow a sequence of five rules:

FIVE STEPS TO TIGHT-QUARTERS FLYCASTING:
1. Choose the best possible position from which to initiate the cast.
2. Make sure your terminal tackle is free and ready for action.
3. Concentrate on potential obstructions *while* you make the cast.
4. Try hard to hit the target on the very first attempt.
5. Don't overfish individual pieces of water.

Look and think *before* the cast. The position from which you choose to launch the fly determines the kinds of casts which are feasible. Your position also defines the degree of difficulty involved and hence the chances of making the presentation successfully. This position is also going to impact on the relative risk of spooking the fish via a dragging fly, getting snagged, or being seen, etc.

In the practice of creekcraft it becomes apparent that stalking and casting are not really separate activities. They are much more a functional whole. Cramped confines force stalking and casting into lockstep like the two parts of a hinge. The stalk produces a platform for the cast and as such each cast is predicated upon a stalk. A bolder or more crafty and imaginative approach to a target can turn an impossible casting situation into a piece of cake.

Clear the Decks

While this problem may be unique to me, I am prone to initiate casts when the leader is looped around the rod tip, the fly is hooked under a nearby twig, or perhaps the line is wrapped around one leg. In tight situations aborted casts ruin a lot of water. I suggest grasping the leader a few inches from the fly in your non-rod hand. Check to make sure the hook hasn't impaled a caddis case or isn't trailing a strand of vegetation. Then shake out enough line to reach out to the target, making sure that line and leader are loose and free. Finally check to see that the path of delivery isn't occluded by branches, etc. and that the rod tip won't catch in an overhanging bough. Then you're ready for action. It's a little like a bowhunter on the ready who nocks an arrow. Or more fancifully, while I've not tried whaling, there may be an analogy to the piling up of loose coils of rope before the harpoon is thrown. In any case, this kind of prophylaxis saves me a great deal of grief…when I remember my own advice.

Watch the Trouble

In the process of making a cast I concentrate my gaze not upon the target but upon barriers through which my terminal tackle must pass on its way to its destination. This takes discipline because it's only natural to focus on the water instead. You want to see where the fly lands and what its fate will be. But there's no point in anticipating trout response until the fly has arrived. If it is left dangling somewhere, nothing good can happen. I find that if I specifically watch the trouble spots, I'm less likely to hang up. Once the fly has made it through, it's easy to quickly switch focus to the water. This is like squeezing your torso between two strands of barbed wire in a fence. You watch the wire, not the grass on the other side.

Get the First Cast in

As a rule, the initial presentation has the best chance of attracting a strike. The likelihood of a take on subsequent casts diminishes progressively. I'm sure the reasons are the same as discussed with reference to stalking and false casting. There is the possibility of mishap every time you put the line in the air. I occasionally take a pot shot at a piece of water, and when I miss there's annoyance. Then I'll bear down and do it right. When there is no response I have to acknowledge that this was a warmed-over attempt. I'll never know what might have been.

Don't Over-fish

If you succeed in placing the fly as desired and nothing happens, what then? How many times should you throw into the same piece of water? This is a highly practical question. Just as in selecting targets or deciding how carefully you'll stalk, the number of presentations addressed to an average target helps determine how much water you'll cover. And again there is no exact answer. It makes sense that pieces that read high for quality deserve more attention. A single cast to a tiny pocket of questionable value should be adequate. In the case of a long, sensuous feeding riffle I won't feel right about giving up until my fly has made a half dozen trips or more. As targets increase in surface area, depth, or volume, there is the increasing possibility that the trout may not have noticed your fly. I am also influenced by the reading on my Spook-O-Meter. When there isn't much natural cover and the fish are jumpy, I'll tend to cut down on the number of casts to a given target since the probability that I've ruined the water grows with each successive try. When the water is murky this threat is greatly reduced, while the possibility that my fly was missed is greater. Then I'll go the other way.

We all are influenced by ongoing events. Without trying we remember if most strikes are coming on the first cast. Pretty soon that fact will sneak into your subconscious and there will be a tendency to make fewer casts. Alternatively, if the trout seem to need to be teased and are coming after the second, third, or fourth presentation, you'll intuitively begin to work each target more thoroughly. We've all heard about finicky fish that ignore good and repeated presentations only to hit number 20 like a ton of bricks. In theory these difficult trout are finally led to believe that a hatch is occurring, or they become irritated when the same silly fly comes by so many times. This happens, but usually on larger streams when there is an abundance of food. Most often, if small stream trout are going to take at all, they'll do it at the first opportunity. Be careful about over-fishing when the fish are reluctant. Beware of falling into a comfortable trance. Bemused by the beauty of your surroundings, it's tempting to cast by reflex, over and over, with no particular plan in mind. For whatever reasons, small streams are frequently sprinkled with hot spots scattered between the dead areas. These may be distinctive pieces of water such as little pools or less defined strips of stream. The fact that so much detail and variability is packed into short segments along a creek's course is further encouragement to keep moving.

5
Tackle Modifications for Small Streams

ROD LENGTH

ROD ACTION

MATERIAL

LINE SELECTION

LEADER LENGTH

TIPPET CALIBER

LEADER SPLICES

REELS

Understanding tackle is much easier once you have a clear picture of what is expected of your equipment. This is why I discussed casting in the preceding chapter. As in any endeavor, we choose our tools on the basis of what they need to accomplish. In this instance the tackle train is designed and coordinated to match stream size.

Rod Length

The three critical qualities of a flyrod are its length, its action, and the material from which it is constructed. With respect to length there is a common misconception that needs to be laid to rest first thing: It's only reasonable to assume that small streams should call for short rods. Long rods suggest long casts which are unnecessary in creek casting. Further, a long rod is a nuisance to weave through bankside vegetation. And intuitively, a pole that's nearly as long as a creek is wide doesn't make sense in any case. In reality, the advantages offered by a rod of reasonable length, say 8 feet or more, far outweigh any inconveniences. In essence a flyrod is a catapult arm. Its projectile is the line. Simple principles of physics state that a longer arm provides a mechanical advantage. This advantage explains why most of the casts described in the preceding chapter are easier to perform and control with longer rods. The

crispness of a roll cast is dependent upon the amount of loading plus the length of the rod. In steeple casting a longer rod throws the line higher just as it will throw a bigger curve and sling more slack. A rod of substantial length is ever so much better for funny casts such as the bow and arrow or pendulum swings. Equally important is avoidance of drag caused by line that's in or on the water just beyond the rod. As we have said, this caboose of the tackle train is apt to get caught by busy, bustling currents and miniature waterfalls that are so common along creeks. Trapped in the toils of these tiny flows, the rear slack soon pulls the leader taut with trout-terrifying drag. The solution is primordial: Lift the line off the surface! Currents can't torment what they can't catch, and a long rod lifts off more line than a short one. A longer lift-off translates into precious seconds of extra drag-free drift and enhances the possibility of a take. Apart from defeating the drag problem, a longer rod actually offers the opportunity to fish with just the leader in the water at very close range. This is the ultimate in tackle finesse.

It's surprising how much influence even 6 inches of rod length has on performance. Whether lifting off slack or casting, a change of less than 10 percent is noticeable. Two rods that vary by a foot in length are distinctively different fishing tools. If this is true, why not choose a shorter rod, which you effectively lengthen by extending your arm when making a cast? Lifting and straightening your arm is a logical way of making the rod longer. Unfortunately, there are some anatomical problems with this approach. It turns out that your wrist and elbow joints are essential members of the casting team. An extended arm appended to the rod butt like an extra segment makes a good rod into a poor one. In this position neither joint functions smoothly and both become stiff. Beyond this, rod stretching gets to be terribly tedious and tiring during a long day. I do sometimes shift my hand position to alter rod length slightly. To squeak the tip under a bough my fingers might creep momentarily onto the barrel above the grip. Or to add a few inches I might slide my hand down onto the reel seat, if only for a cast or two. Nonetheless, it's much better to come equipped with a rod of adequate length at the top of the show. My small stream rods range from 8 to 9½ feet with but one exception. I'll sometimes fish a little 7-footer when the water is high and roily and I can get right on top of the trout. The high water forces me out into the thick and thorny where the shorter rod is welcome and I don't need much of a catapult arm.

Rod Action

There are two extremes of action—fast and slow. Fast rods are relatively stiff, flex primarily in their tip sections, and are possessed of considerable power for throwing heavy lines and propelling casts into the wind. Slow rods flex well down toward the butt to yield a buggy whip sensation and are gifted with great sensitivity. Like an elongate finger, the rod feels as if it were a continuation of your arm. There is marvelous communication with the terminal tackle. Fast rods communicate too, but only after they have been brought to life by a good length of flying line. Otherwise they are a bit rigid and numb in the hand. Since power and distance are not required in creek casting, whereas touch is vital, the two job descriptions for rod action clearly favor the slower end of the spectrum.

In the old days a rod's action was printed directly on the barrel, whether fast, slow, or medium. Now the information is offered less directly through line weight numbers, which indicate the heft of the line best suited for the rod in question. Taken alone these numbers give little indication of action because rod length figures in as well. For a given length, rods that respond to lighter lines display slower action and those that require heavier lines, faster action. Or for a given line weight, the shorter the rod, the faster, and the longer the rod, the slower its action. Even knowing a rod's length and suggested line weight, you still can't predict action with complete assurance. The builder has considerable leeway. Further, graphite rods are usually stiffer and faster than fiberglass rods of corresponding length that are designed to take the same line. To simplify matters, I'd choose a rod that has a pleasing flex well down into the shaft under only gentle urging.

Rod Material

Some years ago it was customary to compare the relative merits of bamboo, fiberglass, and graphite. Today there's little point in such a discussion. Bamboo rods have been priced off the practical market. Meanwhile I fear for the future of fiberglass rods based on merchandising trends. This is too bad, because glass rods are inexpensive and have pleasing action for small stream fishing. However technology has advanced to a point where graphite is lighter, stronger, and more resourceful—and at a very competitive price. Graphite is unique stuff. Graphite rods have amazingly rapid recoil characteristics and put tremendous zing into a flying line, almost as if the fibers were alive and energizing the rod beyond the caster's input. The resilient recoil and leaping line delivery take some getting used to on small water. There is a tendency to overshoot targets, and graphites with other than softish action don't throw slack well. This is especially true of graphites shorter than 8 feet, even those that take light lines. My favorite all-around rod for big water is an 8½-foot graphite that takes a 6- or medium-weight line. That rod is highly versatile and serves me well except on small streams. At close range it's poker stiff. Nonetheless, my best rod for creek casting is also an 8½-foot graphite, but this time for a 4-weight line. Its action is much softer. Graphites are also gusty wind fighters and great companions when it's necessary to fight the battle of the blow. In addition to this rod the others I use most for creek casting are an 8-foot fiberglass rod for 5-weight line and a 9-foot graphite that also likes a 3-weight line. You can't go far wrong with a rod of 8 to 9 feet that takes a relatively light line and communicates comfortably with your hand.

Line Selection

The weight of a flyline's first 30 feet determines its number. This holds for any and all lines, floating or sinking, tapered or level. The system has uniform applicability. The weight number assigned to a given rod is not absolute, however, or cast in bronze. Many rods are designed to take either of a pair of lines, for instance 5-weight/6-weight. Nevertheless, I'd be careful not to *underload* a rod for small stream casting. Underloading will give you the sensation of casting with a broomstick that has a length of floppy string tied to the end. *Overloading* on the other hand has definite value for close-range casting. Line numbers are assigned on the assumption that casts of average length will be made. Admitting that I don't know how "average" is defined, the distance would appear to be in the order of 35 to 45 feet. The point is that creek casts are commonly less than half this long and may include just a few feet of line. You can see that the load which the rod actually feels is a combination of the intrinsic weight of the line plus the length of line that's out and working. Therefore, when an unusually small amount of line is in play, loading will be less than "normal." Simply, this deficit can be corrected in part by increasing line weight. I find that my tackle performs much better at close range with a line that's one or several numbers heavier than my rod calls for. This really comes across with double tapered lines. The business end is thinnest and lightest so short throws of tapered line accentuate underloading. At the same time double tapers are excellent for small streams due to the precision and delicacy with which they deliver a fly. They are also great for roll casting because the loading line that's lifted off the water is heavier than the tip which it must pull. I routinely overload when fishing a double taper at short range.

Here is a suggestion that is useful for small stream fishing and saves money too: Wear in any line is accentuated at the tip since this portion is forced to play crack-the-whip on every cast. The tip becomes flaccid, checked, roughened, and dirty. Floating line ends also lose their buoyancy. I like to trim back these used ends a few inches at a time. With a tapered line this eventually increases the casting weight. However this is not a practical problem. Using these lines on a continuing basis, I know exactly how a given line will perform. Of course with a double taper you first have the option of merely reversing the ends, but eventually this trimming back process will add years of useful small stream life to a line. (I don't use weight forward or rocket tapers for creek casting since they are designed for distance, cost as much as double tapers, and have only one tapered end to begin with.) Trimmed, stubby tapers may lose some of their finesse, but they are still fine for roll casting. Besides, the heavier line end helps with fly control. We tend to assume that if there is enough energy in the tackle train to get the line and leader to do our bidding, the fly will follow along in docile fashion. Weighted wet flies and bulky hair winged dry flies are exceptions. A weighted nymph that tips the scales at a half gram (or a split shot clinched to the leader) requires a fair amount of encouragement if it is to come along cleanly, particularly if the fly is a foot or so beneath the surface. When the fly and/or shot drag their feet, the cast is likely to be short and off line. The same applies to large, fluffy floaters in a stiff breeze. You'll need substantial thrust to drive the fly to its destination in either situation. A reasonably heavy line will assist in a forceful delivery thanks to its greater inertia. I really have nothing against level lines, for that matter. They are inexpensive and their less gentle presentation doesn't matter when the surface is choppy or the water is discolored. In creek casting you shouldn't have to show the line to the trout anyway since target areas are small. Please understand that I don't recommend overloading when longer casts are the order of the day. You can feel the rod lug and say "ouch." The line begins to dip, swoop, and droop as your deliveries lose force and accuracy. Thus I try to be selective with overloading. Sometimes a compromise is necessary. Creeks with stretches of swift pocket water separated by ponded still water requiring long throws are tough to fish with just one line.

I rarely work small streams with a sinking line. In order to drag the fly down to a desired depth, the line has to get down first. Abbreviated casts seldom put enough line in the water for long enough to accomplish this task. (Methods for sinking flies in creek fishing are discussed in chapter 6.) Actually there is a good reason for choosing a floating line when fishing a sunken fly natural drift. Under conditions of difficult visibility created by patches of deep shade or surface glare, the end of a floating line is invaluable as a strike indicator. When the leader disappears, as it surely will, the line end is what you have left to watch, and the closer to the surface, the better. If you've put your line where the trout can see it, you're probably in trouble, so I don't worry about line camouflage. A light-colored line that's easy to see is much the best for fishing a wet fly upstream.

Leader Length

Of the four links in a tackle train—rod, line, leader, and fly—the leader plays the role of Cinderella. No one gets very excited about the skinny little leader, sitting pale and limp in the chimney corner. Nonetheless, the leader influences the preformance of the entire train. The leader's job is to provide camouflage by separating the end of the line from the fly. Theoretically, the longer and thinner the leader, the better the camouflage. Among flyfishing intelligentsia there is a tendency to regard the length of an angler's leader as commensurate with his degree of skill and sophistication. One morning I crossed the threshold of a fancy tackle shop in Aspen with the intention of purchasing some 6-foot leaders for two youngsters I was taking up Hunter Creek. The clerk, a confident young man, greeted my request with an icy stare. Quoth he: "Sir, we recommend 12-foot leaders and have never carried anything shorter than a few in 9-foot lengths." Fortunately the local drug store catered to the needs of more ordinary anglers. This is a typical example of preoccupation with the long leader. Regardless of how skillful you may be, it's fair to state that long leaders such as 12-footers and beyond aren't particularly easy to manage. Like the line, the

leader is thrown by the rod. As an extension of the line, it is a projectile too. The difficulty is that the leader is nearly weightless, and except for the butt end, also spineless. This combination of lightness and limpness makes longer leaders difficult to control. They are particularly vulnerable to wind. Mischievous zephyrs are apt to gust right in the middle of a cast, causing the fly to end up in unexpected places. We run scared trying to guess what the breeze will do. The small stream angler has a second and unique problem: the gossamer leader doesn't begin to do its share with rod loading. For a cast of given length, the longer the leader, the less the loading weight. Consider that no matter the length of cast, the entire leader gets thrown out there every time, all of it. By contrast the length of line is adjusted to fit the distance between the angler and his target. Since leader length is a constant and line length is a variable, it follows that the ratio between the two changes with the length of the cast. Say you're throwing the fly 50 feet at the end of a 9-foot leader. I'd guess that the extended leader plus the forward pointing rod would account for about 14 feet, and the rest of the distance or about 36 feet would be spanned by the line. So 36 feet of line to 9 feet of leader is a ratio of 4 to 1, line to leader. Now cut the cast in half. At 25 feet the reach of the rod plus leader will still cover about 14 feet, leaving a little less than this length of line in the cast, or a ratio of less than 1 to 1. If the cast were further reduced to 18 feet, a common range for creeks, you'd be working with only 4 or 5 feet of line and a 1 to 3 ratio. Try this short throw with a 9-foot leader. Even if the rod is limber and the line is heavy enough to activate it, you won't like the way the rig feels and performs. There will be just too much leader. Whipping nearly pure monofilament about is very much like whistling in the breeze. Thus, the length of your leader has increasing impact on tackle performance as casts grow shorter.

Let's get back to Hunter Creek and the 12-foot leaders. Like many mountain streams, Hunter is swift and flat with scattered rock pockets and small pools near bends in the channel. Its brook trout are particularly fond of narrow strips of slack water up against the banks. The creek is heavily willow thatched, and this means that those strips are partially roofed over. This calls for short, sidearm casts. A 6-foot leader affords precise control without spooking sentinels and is sufficient to span the entirety of most targets. It may be that the tackle shop's disdain for leaders of less than 12 feet was a tacit suggestion that real flyfishers don't fool with little "cricks." Nonetheless, I know guides on Montana's Bighorn and Beaverhead rivers who are expert at extracting lunkers with leaders as short as 3 feet! One thing's for sure, the trout won't discriminate against you on the basis of the length of your leader. I think of leaders as wayward children, and the longer, the more likely they are to misbehave. Twelve-footers can't wait to ring the bell on you in the event of some minor casting error. If you believe that the longer the leader, the greater the potential for grief, and if you agree with my view as to what a leader is for (I exclude impressing your peers), it would seem reasonable to choose a leader that's long enough to satisfy needs for camouflage, but no longer. A good small stream rule of thumb is that the leader should roughly match the rod's length minus 6 inches to a foot or so. Practically, this means having more line out and working than leader. According to this formula, the leaders that I use for 90 percent of my small stream fishing range from 4 feet up to 9 feet. Functionally, this range is surprisingly broad, for you can detect subtle changes in the performance of your tackle chain based on differences of as little as 6 inches. I make an exception to this rule when casting a great deal of slack is important. Added leader can prolong drag-free drift because the monofilament is far more adept at falling in compressed squiggles than is the end of the line. This piling up of the leader has been called "puddling," and long leaders puddle best. In fact leaders of 20 feet and more have been used for this purpose on big water. Unsightly though the puddle mess may be, the current must drain most of the puddle before it can distort the fly's drift. So this is really a matter of trading more difficult cast control for enhanced protection against drag. On small streams I merely try to cast smaller puddles, and a 9-footer is usually plenty long enough.

During high water abbreviated casts with a line overload and short leader make sense.

Tippet Caliber

Tippet caliber is the second critical quality in leader selection. The thinness of a tippet enhances camouflage and also limpness. The latter is important in obtaining the most natural drift of a floating or sunken fly. Several considerations limit the extent to which a tippet can be whittled down. Precise placement of a fly is more difficult with a fine tippet, especially if the fly is either heavy or bulky. Understandably, wind makes things worse and can blow a big dry fly around like a kite. In the X system of grading tippet caliber, only one one-thousandth of an inch in tippet diameter separates individual grades. Regardless, a change of just one tippet caliber is functionally important. So often I find myself getting by with a certain tippet yet struggling with the tackle and missing targets by just a little. I can almost always set things straight by increasing the tippet diameter by one X value. A tippet/fly combination that's working nicely may also become unmanageable when the breeze comes up. Again a jump of one caliber should help.

Tensile strength diminishes with tippet caliber too, although modern synthetics are amazingly tough. While small stream trout don't generally threaten to tear up tackle, they have an excellent opportunity to hang your leader. Creeks are very snaggy places. Once anchored, as around a willow root, even a smallish fish can snap a tender tippet or tear out your hook. It's very helpful to have a tippet that's strong enough to permit you to apply some pressure before they hang you up. If you can keep trout away from dangerous structures such as submerged clumps of brush, roots, or log jams you'll lose many fewer fish. Larger trout can virtually scissor thin tippets when they roll and slash. In situations where the trout are sizable a stouter tippet makes sense.

In the following paragraphs I've attached descriptive comments for each of the five tippets I fish most on small streams.

2X: This is a coarse tippet. I use 2X for purposes of controlling heavy nymphs or streamers. This usually means early-season outings or when storms have created runoff-like conditions. At 8 pounds-plus test strength, 2X handles anything up to tarpon.

3X: 3X is a bit on the stout side for small streams, but is an excellent choice for wet flies other than the real juggernauts. I also like the substance or body of a 3X tippet for large dry flies, as when stone flies are about in early summer and otherwise for windy dry fly fishing.

4X: This is the most useful caliber, overall. 4X handles dry flies from #12s to #16s nicely and is a good tippet for smaller wet flies. Tensile strength should be ample and 4X also gives you decent camouflage plus a good degree of limpness for natural drifts.

5X: A fairly delicate tippet, 5X fits a #16 or #18 dry fly beautifully and is a good choice for tiny wet flies. 5X does get pushed around by any sort of breeze and requires some care and consideration when setting the hook. I fish 5X a good deal after mid-season when the water drops and clears.

6X: I used to be afraid to fish wispy 6X because I broke it so often. No more. The newest tippet materials give 6X almost the same tensile strength as the 4X leaders of yore. (Close to 3 lbs.) This caliber is well suited for midges tied on #20 hooks and smaller.

As you can see, adjusting leader length and tippet caliber are separate means of fine tuning your terminal tackle. The two can work toward the same end. For example, when cover is sparse and the trout are spooky, a relatively longer, finer leader makes sense. Or when wind is a problem, a shorter leader and heavier tippet will surely help. But you can also mix length and tippet caliber in a contrasting way. It was once impossible to buy leaders that were both short and fine. Fortunately this is no longer the case, since this blend is very useful for small streams. This sort of leader has finesse, and yet cast control is still acceptable thanks to shortness. I will emphasize again that minor changes in either length or tippet caliber make a difference. Given that you have both to play with, the opportunities for leader design are almost limitless. Having considered the physical layout of the creek, the water and wind conditions, the size of the trout, and the nature of the flies you wish to offer, you can construct a comprehensive length/tippet formula that best fits the need.

Leader Splices

The ability to tie a leader splice knot is an integral skill in flyfishing. With this knot you can replace tippets that have been shortened through changing flies or weakened by wear or wind knots. Splicing also makes it possible to tailor leaders to lengths that are in between the lengths that are available commercially. This option is valuable for tight-quarters casting where tackle performance is so sensitive to leader specifications. Tippet replacement is almost a necessity with knotless, tapered leaders unless you are prepared to just throw them away after a few fly changes. These leaders taper very steeply at the tip. Thus after 4 to 6 inches have been trimmed from a new 7½-footer tapered to 4X, you will be fishing a 3X tippet. Take off another few inches and you'll be working with 2X. And although wind knots are supposedly the result of inept casting (euphemistically related to accidents caused by the wind), these little beasts come to grace the leaders of all of us, both great and small. These simple overhand knots weaken a tippet by one X value or more. If a tippet that's beset by a wind knot breaks, the break will almost always occur at the knot. So you can either opt to ignore the creatures or replace your tippet. It's a gamble, and like replacing your oil filter, it's up to you.

Getting back to odd lengths, let's say you want a leader with a 3X tippet that's intermediate between the standard 6-foot and 7½-foot lengths. Just splice 10 inches of 3X tippet material to the end of a "store bought" 6-footer that tapers to 2X. (Trimming is seldom necessary, since normal wear and tear automatically creates shortened leaders or leader bases to which tippets can be added.) There are several splice knots, of which the most popular is variously known as the Barrel, Blood, or Fisherman's Knot. This knot is highly reliable. With a little practice it can be tied in 30 seconds (unless someone is watching, your fingers are cold, or the trout are rising). My only problems with slippage have come when my fingers had a little silicone floatant on them that got into the knot. It is necessary, though, that the Barrel be tied properly. I know a fellow who had terrible problems with this knot and grew so frustrated that he took to adding a drop of super glue from a tube he carried in his vest. Everything was fine until one day when he glued his thumb and forefinger together almost permanently. A 25-yard spool of top-grade tippet material costs no more than a leader, and since a full set, 2X through 6X, will nest snugly in a small pocket, replacing tippets is just common sense.

Incidentally, slower-action rods are also helpful in reducing the frequency of snapped tippets. Broken tippets are most commonly the result of an overly zealous attempt to set the hook. You lose the fish, your fly, and your temper. The tippet may need to be replaced as well, so it's not an occasion for rejoicing. If you share my occasionally heavy-handed hook setting proclivities, you'll find that the whip in a slower rod damps out much of the shattering force of a strike.

I hope you'll agree that the leader should not be treated as the Cinderella of your tackle chain. She deserves at least equal status with any other link. And if Cinderella comes cheap, so much the better!

Reels

The reel is not a very imaginative piece of equipment. In essence a reel is a garage for unoccupied line. Because small stream fishing is especially traumatic to tackle, I prefer a reel that is inexpensive and durable. When I was about ten my father gave me an automatic reel—I'm not sure just why. As a result I grew up "spring loaded," so to speak. Today the automatic has become the pariah of flyfishing paraphernalia, and yet it offers certain advantages, at least in creekcraft. I don't think it's fair to damn the automatic across the board. The two major raps against the spring loaders have to do with weight and supposedly complicated, gimmicky construction. Automatics are undeniably heavy, about 10 ounces, and thus several times the weight of a standard single-action reel. This changes the feel of a light rod. I grew up in an era when 5-ounce rods were common. Like Wagnerian divas, those sturdy tools of yesteryear were so hefty that an automatic clinging to their skirts was hardly noticed. The people who make and sell rods have a tendency to endow their products with certain sensuous properties to be enjoyed and applauded by the angler's hand as he orchestrates symphonious casts with his baton. Theoretically an automatic, like a lump of lead, causes the baton to conduct a dreadful dirge instead. The reel, of course, is centered below the hand with the working, feeling parts of the rod well above where they can hardly be influenced. As to the gimmicky charge, like any reel automatics need to be kept free of dirt and sand. This isn't a problem, since they are easily cleaned, and I have rarely experienced a serious malfunction. An automatic's cage is actually harder to dent and deform than that of a lighter, single-action reel. The good thing about the spring loaders is that they pick up line almost instantaneously. You don't have to crank up slack every time you move to a new position. Most anglers are right-handed and most prefer the reel handle on the right side. This means switching hands every time you put line back on the spool—and switching back again. The alternative of letting slack trail behind while cruising up a creek isn't a wise one. An automatic also keeps tension on the line when playing a trout. This frees your other hand. I've met people who believe that an automatic pulls the fish right in, thereby depriving the angler of his hard-earned enjoyment. This is silly. The luxury of a free hand isn't silly at all, though, when trying to chase down a good trout in a swift, slick-bottomed creek. This means stone hopping, log leaping, and brush dodging. That extra hand is great for steadying yourself in the process of clambering over a felled tree or grasping a branch while skidding through a slippery spot. And there's no loose line to trip over. Still, the automatic runs countercurrent to modern tackle sophistication. I too generally fish a single action, but in certain situations I still break out one of the old spring loaders. I figure that a man's reel is like his religion and politics!

6
Flies for Small Water

Flies for Small Water

There's no point in debating the comparative merits of dry flies versus wet flies. Both are essential to success. Each has its own set of roles. Purists, whether dry fly or wet, never realize the success they might have otherwise enjoyed. I will discuss dry flies first for reasons that are practical rather than based upon preference.

Dry Flies

I'm convinced that beginners maintain interest longer and build confidence faster fishing a dry fly. Like playing with boats, it's fun to watch them float along. Besides, whether tyro or veteran, a surface fly is much the easiest to follow. You can see a dry fly alight, track its drift, watch for correctable drag, and hopefully set the hook if there is a take. In small stream fishing where targets are tiny and precision placement is vital, at times it's simply more efficient to fish on top. Still another practical consideration comes into play when creeks are low and choked with water weed. A floater won't run aground on you, whereas "de-gooing" a wet fly after nearly every cast is a bothersome waste of time.

It has been said that trout take only a small proportion of their food from the surface. However this has little to do with their willingness to rise when an inviting morsel drifts through their topside windows. It's a critical observation that trout will attack dry flies when

there is no evidence whatever of natural insects on the surface or of spontaneous rises. To my chagrin I occasionally forget this. I once had a spectacular day on a certain creek fishing nymphs in the early season. By design I returned the following year on the identical date. Through wishful thinking I suppose, I had an eerie feeling of being transported back in time that morning. Everything was familiar, the water, the weather, the very look and smell of the place. Intuitively, I tied on the same nymph pattern and even entered the stream where I had begun the year before. There was one difference, though. By midafternoon I had hooked three fish, landing one 7-incher. I was still enjoying myself, but like you I'd rather catch fish than not—and I was clearly not. About then these mental mists began to clear enough for me to realize that I had yet to work the surface. During the final two hours, a dry fly caught 13 trout for me, two of them sizable, despite the continuing absence of any spontaneous rises or food forms on the surface that I could see. The point is that unless the water is nearly opaque, you can't know what the trout will do about dry flies until you try. It doesn't take long to find out.

Dry Fly Patterns

I have three suggestions:

1. Choose patterns with broad, general appeal to trout rather than specific "hatch matchers."
2. Include flies that suggest terrestrial insects.
3. Depend upon a small number of patterns in which you have confidence.

Creeks support the same insects that are found in rivers. It follows that there will be similar hatches. However, on small freestone streams these events are less frequent, of briefer duration, and less intense than on big water. As a consequence trout in small streams are seldom terribly selective in terms of demanding precise, matching patterns. When a hatch does come along, often just a scattering of naturals appears and for only a few minutes, such that neither I nor the trout become particularly aroused. I'm really not an anti–hatch matcher (or anti-intellectual). It's just that less-focused patterns are so much more practical overall. Even if you do encounter a heavy hatch and rise and are equipped with the proper matching pattern, there's no guarantee that the trout won't treat your offering with contempt. Uneducated, ill-mannered fish of this sort are referred to as "difficult." Oddly enough, these same difficult trout may very well fall prey to a non-matching pattern that merely gives *an impression* of an edible and which hardly resembles the naturals to which they are rising. The value of these impressionistic patterns is inestimable from the standpoint of plain economy. Stocking your fly boxes and keeping track of what's where, how many are left, and in which hook size is both simpler and less expensive if you have only a handful of reliable patterns to inventory. The compulsive hatch matcher has to lug around a virtual menagerie of special flies against each potential need. And if no hatch develops, there may not be enough hours in the day to test this potpourri of patterns. I should know, for I was once in the habit of carrying over 70 patterns with me in various corners of my jackets. (I wore two simultaneously in the manner of an ambulatory tackle shop.)

Starting to discuss specific patterns of this type is like taking a whack at the tar baby, so I will mention just two. The rather gaudy Royal Coachman and more subdued Adams have long and outstanding track records across the country. While a list of popular impressionistic patterns would number in the dozens, you could do worse than to fish these two.

Terrestrial insects make a particular contribution to the welfare of both the trout and the anglers who frequent small streams. The reason relates to the bank's function as a source of food and the magnification of this factor when two such platforms are in close apposition. The grasshopper, ant, beetle, caterpillar, and others of their kith and kin continually fall into the water. Occasionally they appear in spates, as during a mating flight of ants, or during a bout of breeze when hoppers are rife, but artificials that suggest terrestrial food forms are a good bet at any time. The Irresistibles and Humpies are two popular series of dry flies with a buggy, terrestrial look. Irresistibles are tied with bodies of clipped, shaped hair. Humpies feature hair fibers folded over atop the hook shank with the free ends forming tails and wings. Body, hackle, and wing color are varied to create a number of subpatterns. The common denominator is the silhouette of a plump body suggestive of a beetle, cricket, hopper, or whatever. More to the point, these flies are consistently productive. One of my favorite small stream terrestrials is an ant imitation tied with nothing more than black thread and dyed deer hair. In the surface film this primitive fly displays a provocative silhouette that triggers trout response built upon familiarity with this ever-present food form. Small stream trout will almost always rise to an ant if they are willing to come up at all. Other terrestrial patterns such as hopper imitations, Irresistibles, and Humpies are also easy to see on the water. So are hair-winged dry flies such as the Royal Wulff, essentially a Royal Coachman with hair wings, and the Golden Adams (an Adams tied with gold hair wings).[5]

Admitting that most of us will want to fish more than just one or two flies and that a certain amount of testing is usually ongoing, having confidence in a small cadre of favorite patterns is important. An angler and his fly are very much a team. He needs to have faith in his feathered friend on the far end of the leader. When I doubt that my fly is going to do its part, the edge

---

[5]William C. Black, *Hooked on Flies* (Tulsa: Winchester Press, 1980), pp. 19–29.

comes off my concentration. Certainly pleasurable anticipation is dulled.

Before dispensing with matching patterns too cavalierly, *spring creeks* deserve special mention. While not necessarily small streams, spring creeks are distinctive fisheries that display a consistent set of qualities. On the basis of their origin, these include stable water level and temperature, relative alkalinity, and extensive growth of underwater vegetation. As a by-product, spring creeks nourish tremendous quantities and varieties of insect life, not to mention more exotic delectables such as freshwater shrimp, snails, minnows, leaches, etc. Visibility for the trout is excellent since the water is typically clear and smooth of surface. Spring creek trout tend to be correspondingly selective, demanding pretty exact imitations of the food forms to which they are rising. These fortunate fish find themselves in the midst of a natural cornucopia. Surrounded by *à la carte* shrimp and escargot, they act like overfed gourmets. So when a blizzard-like hatch develops, it's not surprising that these trout are picky and hard to please. Hatch matching may be a frank necessity and becomes a challenge. These super fisheries are beloved by sophisticated flyfishers and achieve the status of flowing legends. It's interesting, though, that even spring creek trout with Ph.Ds can be suckered with impressionistic patterns. My wife has Idaho relatives who have fished Silver Creek near Sun Valley for decades. Silver is one of the best known of all spring creeks, and its myriad mayfly hatches come off like clockwork. However my in-laws grew up before hatch matching came into vogue. Their angling habits were already firmly established. To my surprise I found that while they stalked individual trophy fish, they paid scant attention to hatches. They depended instead on a #12 Irresistible! They would fish this rather coarse fly in the face of any old hatch, say a cloud of #22 mayflies. The huge rainbows and browns that they captured put fancier flyfishers to shame. My unpretentious in-laws firmly believed that if that Irresistible was put in the right place, in the right way, and at the right time it would get the job done. While more scientific anglers were feverishly searching through their boxes for the right fly, Uncles Hank and Roy and Aunt Verda were just fishing away. It occurred to me that they enjoyed considerable peace of mind by not having to worry about hatch matching.

Food-filled spring creeks promise selective trout.

While Silver Creek is not a narrow stream, its overhanging, grassy banks are eminently buggy. This probably explains the fat-bodied Irresistible's success. However, banks can also concentrate the adults of aquatic species in ways that are useful to small stream flyfishers. Adult caddis and stone flies typically frequent bankside vegetation from which they flutter out over the water to the delight of vigilant trout. My son Charlie and I really cashed in on this phenomenon along the headwaters of the Chama River in Colorado in late June. We hoped that the runoff had abated, but I parked the truck at the end of the road with growing concern, for banks of blinding snow were still annealed to the face of Banded Peak at the head of the basin. We climbed to the crest of a ridge, where we were rewarded by a vista of the nascent river performing a spectacular free-fall from Banded's sheer side. It was calendar art and a welcome excuse for breath catching. Then we dropped down from the high trail, listening for the cry of the baby river below. I remember thinking that we heard its crowing too soon and that the call was too loud. My fears were soon confirmed. The Chama raced and foamed, tearing at alder roots well up on its banks and reading at only 48 degrees. Fishing wet, we'd be in the water most of the time, with the promise of aching toes plus the probability of chilled, disinterested trout. It's always nice to be wrong about gloomy predictions. As Charlie and I pushed along we were pelted from all sides by big stone flies, many of them landing clumsily on our jackets. Stone flies are sometimes called Willow Flies in recognition of their love of the streamside greenery. Whether courting, mating, egg laying, or just cavorting, stonies love to flutter capriciously just above the water, sometimes dragging their landing gears. Ninety percent of the holding water was up against the Chama's banks, and so were 90 percent of the stone flies. It was just a matter of chucking a large dry fly into any washbasin's worth of holding and bang! In that current a 13-inch brown trout became a ferocious fighter, leading to a series of frantic, skidding downstream chases, rod bent double. By afternoon my legs issued complaints of cruel and unusual punishment based on charges of fatigue plus immersion frostbite. Charlie and I had released some 70 trout by then, though, so I didn't listen with too much sympathy. The few brownies that we cleaned

for supper had been gorging on stone flies, as expected. We were lucky this day, because stone fly activity is transient. The adults had just hatched, probably a day or so before, and would soon begin mating and ovipositing. Then they would be gone until the next year.

When caddis are doing the bankside fluttering, the Elk Hair Caddis is an excellent choice. Like the ant imitation, this well-known pattern depends upon an impressionistic silhouette. The Elk Hair Caddis is easy to see on the water too, always a bonus on small streams.

A simple but effective ant imitation and an Elk Hair Caddis.

Fly Size

Since finding your fly on the water is important, I like to fish fairly sizable artificials. The trout, however, may prefer petite patterns. Their vote wins. The "strike to hook ratio" is a way to test these preferences. In fishing a fly on the surface, it's usually possible to observe strikes or rises. A certain proportion of these risers will be hooked. The rest either flee or return to their holds. Thus, a ratio of rises to hooked fish can be calculated. If every fish that takes gets hooked, the ratio is 1 to 1. If half the risers are impaled, the ratio is 2 to 1, and so on. Each strike brings a twinge of excitement, but when ratios are high there is frustration too. While it's not reasonable to expect to achieve a 1 to 1 ratio over any protracted span, if the trout are taking deeply and with confidence you can come close, say 9 hooked out of every 10 takes. The other side of the coin is what I call "hot ironing." This means a lightning-quick attack on the fly followed instantaneously by a frenzied retreat—like testing the surface of an iron with wetted finger. This is the sort of reception you'd like to avoid, for when trout are hot ironing, ratios can easily climb to 10 to 1. This has absolutely nothing to do with slow reflexes either.

As dry fly fishing goes, a ratio of 2 to 1 isn't bad. When the ratio gets up toward 3 to 1, I try to improve things. I begin by changing to a smaller fly in the same pattern, assuming that the pattern that's in use has been eliciting a reasonable number of strikes to begin with. Imagine that a #12 fly has attracted roughly 20 rises, hooking only 4 fish for a 5 to 1 ratio. You now tie on a #14, setting the hook in the jaw of 5 of the next 10 customers. Hypothetically this 2 to 1 ratio ought to essentially double your catch so long as the strikes keep coming. Then you might want to try a #16 in an effort to drive the ratio down further. I have seldom seen improvement that resulted from changing to a larger hook size unless the trout were after an insect that was significantly larger than my artificial. You'll agree that any measurable increase in your fly's credibility rating is worth the tradeoff in somewhat poorer visibility. Just as small stream trout tend not to be terribly selective for pattern, they are seldom picky about fly size when they come up for a look-see. But looking a floating fly over and taking it with sincerity are by no means the same thing. My log book is filled with accounts of days when I could get plenty of rises to flies as large as #12s or as small as #18s in a given pattern and yet my actual catch was still very much dependent upon hook caliber. You will usually find that there is no additional gain in dropping below a certain hook size. If there were a direct correlation between smaller ratios and smaller hooks, I suppose we'd all fish #28s and all suffer from terrible eyestrain. The reality is different, so I go with the size that earns the lowest ratio.

Changing patterns is the obvious next move. Here I turn to another method for testing sincerity. The plain Black Ant pattern that I've mentioned earlier is almost always taken with assurance if the fish are at all enthusiastic. In fact the Ant sometimes runs up a ratio of less than 1 to 1! This happens when the fish hook themselves after I've lost sight of the fly. I'll lift the line for a new cast to find a trout tugging on the other end, a hooked fish without a visible strike. This isn't uncommon. The Ant is dark and floats half submerged in the surface film, so it's easy to miss. Meanwhile, the trout seem to have such relaxed confidence that they mouth the Ant and just swim off with it. Whatever, the ratio I get with the Ant is my gold standard. (A simple Beetle tied in almost the same way is equally effective, and I like both in sizes 14, 16, and 18.) I don't fish these terrestrials routinely because they are so hard to follow on the water. The trout, too, have trouble seeing them in chop or through much roil.

Wet Flies

Never think of the wet fly as a substitute. Wets deserve far better. As with dry flies, you can't know what subsurface flies will accomplish until you give them a chance. At times they are more effective than the floaters in the face of what appears to be ideal dry fly water. And when stream conditions such as heavy currents and cold, roily water do discourage the trout from rising, subsurface feeding is likely to continue unabated and may be accentuated. Thus, we fish wets not instead of, but because! This was brought home to me as a youngster fishing a creek in Colorado's South Park. It was May and I had floated a big dry fly all day with scant success. Eventually I hooked a pansizer in a pool fed by a strong current that churned through a cluster of rocks. There a willow bough had been trapped under the surface. Before I could react, this feisty rainbow streaked upstream under the branches. He rocketed high out of the water, landing back on the downstream side of the bough. I was hopelessly snagged and the victor soon threw the hook. Irritated, I tossed the whole bough out onto the bank to work the mess free. As I knelt, I was startled to see that the deadfall was literally swarming with big stone fly larvae, highly agitated by the threatening environment in which they so suddenly found themselves. I had read that stone fly nymphs require swift water, so this rookery branch was well situated. Just above I came upon a similar spot with submerged driftwood. Sure enough, its branches too were alive with the larvae. As I began to look more carefully, they were drifting everywhere, particularly where currents spilled into quiet water. This tardy discovery paid off in two ways. During the remainder of that afternoon I did well with a large wet fly that resembled the stone fly nymphs.

Secondly, I reasoned that if so many larvae were active, hatching must be imminent. I returned one week later, and sure enough, there they were. This time the same big dry fly that had aroused little interest earlier was just the ticket. The analogy to the good day on the Chama headwaters is obvious. This is a familiar pattern in early season, i.e., nymphs before adults, wet flies before dry flies.

Subaquatic larvae of all types participate in the rites of spring. Mature nymphs that are ready to hatch leave the security of their winter burrows to clamber and scud about. Juveniles become active too as they molt, shucking old skins for new. This heightened activity combined with heavy currents means that larvae get washed free. There is an influx of food that is new in a sense and readily obtainable for the trout.

A heavy summer rain partially recreates the conditions of early season and can create a burst of superlative fishing. Long, hot days virtually sap the life from parched streams, but how quickly a thunderstorm washes the stale, tepid water away. An abundance of edibles gets washed in from the banks, while aquatic larvae set adrift are at the mercy of foraging trout. Take the cased caddis in their buoyant homes of leaf fiber, or the shallow burrowing nymphs of the crane fly and certain of the mayflies. Secure enough in the gentle flows of summer, these dens and backpack domiciles cannot withstand the gouging ravages of a cloudburst. And what of the free-ranging caddis or net builders cowering behind strands of gossamer, the many swimming larvae and tiny minnows accustomed to placid shallows? All must be chaos for them, a violent, disruptive stirring of Nature's fishbowl. Goaded by a rapid influx of food, revived by cool, newly oxygenated water, and shielded by a blanket of roil, it's no surprise that the trout go on a binge. It's banquet time!

The following experience taught me a good lesson about storms and wet flies: A group of friends and I once made an annual trip to a ranch where we could fish either a river or its tributary creek. One morning far away grumblings and groanings from an overcast sky hinted at serious meteorologic indigestion. Toward noon vapid little showers began to mist, like perspiration, as if the system were warming up for some great event. By dark it seemed poised for an Olympian effort. And a grand performance it was, all orchestrated into a cabin-rattling climax toward 2 A.M. A wan and nebulous sun greeted us the next morning, as blurry and sodden as several of our party. The river had not risen as much as we feared, but it had such a grey, unfriendly look that my friend Bill and I opted to try the tributary. Skidding down the mud-slicked trail, I soon wished I had joined the others on the river. Things weren't good, and I managed to make them worse by deciding that it wouldn't much matter how I fished the cocoa currents. I tied on a big hopper imitation, floating it through pockets of slack along the banks where there had been dry land the day before. It wasn't a bad plan, although you'd think a sensible person might have tried something else after an hour without a strike. By noon I had caught two small browns and felt gratified to have dented an impossible situation. We had planned to regroup for a late lunch, so I headed back, finding that the river crew had already arrived. It's not normal for fishermen to quit on time, let alone early, and I guessed the reason. They were skunked. My two fish made me top rod! Bill had not returned, though, and nearly an hour passed before we heard loud stomping and tromping on the porch. With all the mudkicking came another premonition: Bill had killed them! I've noticed so often that when anglers have a poor day there's a tendency to slip into camp unobtrusively, almost as if they hadn't gone astream at all. But after a good day, expect a boisterous return. Again I was right. Bill's answer to the inevitable question was: "I just missed thirty, twenty-eight, or twenty-nine I think." That was bad enough, but he proceeded to nail down the lid with: "And they were almost all nice size." You can guess what the next query must have been: "Just an old fly," our companion replied and it surely was. Tied on a #12 hook, the thing had begun the day as a grey, fur-dubbed nymph with grizzly hackle and tail. Now it looked like something the cat dragged in. (There were no snide remarks, you can be sure.) Bill went on to describe a variety of food forms that he had found when he cleaned his fish— worms, minnows, beetles, and just all kinds of larvae. As far as he could tell, his fly hadn't imitated anything in particular and yet resembled lots of the nymphs in a general way. Bill had cashed in on a massive feeding spree while I, dunce-like, prided myself on two tinies, taken off the surface. Incidentally, Bill started just a half mile above me that morning, so we had been fishing comparable water. It wasn't long before I was back on the creek, retracing Bill's steps and armed with grey nymphs, size 12. I practically licked my chops. The trout, however, had done the same, finished their meals, and turned in for a nap. Easily available food within the creek had become less abundant with dropping water levels and slowing currents. This tale carries a three-pronged message: (1) Don't give up before trying all possible options. (2) Hit by the same storm, a large stream may turn sour while its tributary becomes red hot. (3) Under conditions such as those described, wet flies should prove superior to floaters.

Late season also brings the wet fly to the fore. As water temperatures plummet, trout are less willing to rise and may choose to exercise their prerogative not to come up at all. Besides, most of the significant hatches are over for the year and there is less reason for them to patrol the surface. Torpid though the trout may be, when a succulent wet fly is drifted to them in their holding places, home-delivered, they often take. I've sensed a certain urgency to feed, almost an anxiety, even after the trout were pretty well holed up for the winter. Opportunities to obtain food easily must be few and far between during late season. When a chance to capture some calories comes along, they don't waste it.

Regardless of storm and season there are times when trout feed subsurface for reasons best known to themselves. I once had a notion that dry fly fishing should reach its absolute peak for the year in early fall when the water is still fairly warm. I would carefully restock my supplies of floaters only to find wet fly action to be much better. There is an autumnal phenomenon that I call "Operation Mossballs": In the creeks and rivers of Colorado's San Juan Mountains I have repeatedly caught trout with swollen, hard abdomens as if packed with insects. Instead, when the fish were cleaned I found tight, matted masses of green moss fiber. It is my suspicion that they scarf up the salad stuff from the bottom because it contains quantities of tiny larvae, crustacea, or whatever—like a shrimp salad with lots of lettuce and not so many shrimp. There's a practical aspect, for when Operation Mossballs is ongoing the fish will take a drifted wet fly much more readily than a floating arti-

ficial. A hatch may come along, bringing some surface action, but over the span of a day wets are more productive by far.

Methods of Presentation

The way in which a wet fly is presented is more important in the long run than the pattern. There are two basic options: The artificial may be drifted naturally to the trout, as if there were no line and leader attached, or it may be manipulated, i.e., activated. In my experience those days when the two methods were equally effective have been few. The decision almost always matters. Although there is no reason not to try both options, I have a strong bias for the natural drift on small water. This is because so many food forms are incapable of swimming or do so feebly and are thus carried by the current. Mechanically, the easiest way to fish a fly natural drift is off an upstream cast, whereas "swum" flies are customarily cast across or across and downstream. Since small streams are best fished upstream, natural drifting is a logical approach. I'm convinced that day in and day out, a drifted fly will attract more strikes. Unfortunately, there is a fundamental difficulty attached to fishing a wet fly upstream. Since a fly cannot drift freely on a taut line/leader, there will have to be at least a little slack. This means that when a trout takes there will often be no telltale tap or tug. So how to know when to set the hook? This is a critical question. Strike detection and hook setting while fishing natural drift are the most challenging of all wet fly skills and the acme of satisfaction for the angler who has mastered the techniques. Two stages of accomplishment are involved: The first is an awareness of the signs of a take, what to look for. The second is prompt reaction to the triggering sign.

It is often difficult to see a sunken fly clearly. Accordingly we learn to train our eyes, *without precise focus*, on a bushel-basket-sized area about where the fly is presumed to be. With luck you might see a fish suddenly take your fly. More commonly there is an indescribable impression of movement in the water, for example a darkish shadow or flicker of light. The creek fisher is at an advantage here because he is close to his fly. When casts are longer or there is glare or roil, watching the bushel basket area isn't practical. Then it becomes necessary to focus, *this time sharply*, on that part of the tackle train that's farthest out toward the fly. Most often this will be some part of the leader, possibly a splice knot. If roil or glare is severe, you may end up watching the line/leader splice or tip of the line. The triggering signs of interest are related to *changes* in the behavior of the terminal tackle during the drift. It is important to understand that there is a range of intensity of these changes or indications of a strike. For example a really vicious hit causes the leader/line to dart backwards. That's hard to miss. A less intense signal would be an abrupt stop in the drift, as in skidding to a halt. A mere slowing of the drift would be still more subtle. A related group of changes includes left/right deviation of the path of drift or unexpected sinking of the leader/line. As before, these signals might be abrupt and stark or much less obvious. It follows that almost anyone possessed of reasonable eyesight and alertness will appreciate the flagrant strike signs. Picking up the more subtle reflections is not nearly so easy. This level of sensitivity comes with patience and practice. But it does come, and with it a sense of accomplishment—not to mention larger catches.

The highest degree of awareness is close to mystical. Countless anglers agree that it is not uncommon to react, setting the hook, without knowing why! Stated differently, you can't recall what it was that told you to pull the line tight—even at that very time. Apparently the angler sees something so transient and/or a change so slight that the event never dents his conscious level of recall. Regardless, the stimulus was sufficient to pull the angler's trigger. There have been many days when I've hooked most of my fish without knowing just what it was that set off my subconscious strike sensor. Can you see why this is so much fun? Harking back to the idea of a Spook-O-Meter, you could indicate the spectrum of strike indication intensities on a gauge akin to a speedometer. For every fisherman there would be a point along this range where he would begin to pick up signals of a given intensity. Signals falling below this level would generally go unrecognized. With growing experience that sensitive zone should shift to the left side of the dial.

Strike Indicators

Bits of bright material attached to the leader are helpful in leader watching. On small streams the angler is so close to the action that there is perhaps less need for these aids. Still, it's impossible to make definite statements about strike indicators. So much depends upon circumstances. The quality of lighting, glare, and the length of your casts all enter into the equation. Many flyfishers report that these bright indicators are most useful on longer casts where the visual angle out to the leader is relatively flat. As I suggested earlier, a trout's take may be directly visible in the form of a shadowy movement or flash. In that case it may be best to concentrate on the area where your fly should be rather than upon the leader. Here's an example: I was fishing during the late runoff in clearing water and had placed a quarter-inch sleeve of florescent plastic on the leader some 18 inches above my nymph. Just as soon as the cast was completed, I tried to find the orange dot as quickly as possible. My problem shouldn't have been a problem, for the trout were taking aggressively. However this frequently translated into almost immediate strikes, and these I was missing. I saw all kinds of flashes out of the corner of my eye while frantically searching for the indicator, but invariably too late. This is a frustrating and not uncommon experience. Fortunately you can just ignore the indicator (or remove it) as I did on this occasion, essentially doubling my catch.

The small stream angler can avail himself of several "natural" strike indicators when drifting a fly at close range. The *angle* at which the leader enters/exits the surface will be steep, say 30 degrees or more. The angle itself makes an excellent visual fix point. It becomes an "object" that can be easily found and followed. When a trout interferes with your fly, the angle is likely to either flatten or to change the pace or direction of its drift. A variation on this theme involves rod "lifting." With the fly close at hand it's common practice to keep it bumping along the bottom by *gently* raising the rod tip periodically. Or if the fly does snag, a delicate nudge will usually get it going again. The rod is also raised before making a fresh cast. In any of these situations, if a trout is mouthing the fly when the tip is raised, the angle is liable to open or widen. This is a subtle yet promising signal that encourages an immediate, brisk response in hopes of setting the hook. Incidentally, this type of fly control is greatly facilitated by a rod of reasonable length.

There's still another form of strike indicator that depends upon a trait inherent in leaders. Stored in a coil, the butt ends typically develop memory by retaining a gentle spiral. In the water these sea serpent humps protrude above the surface where they are easily visible. The slightest interference with the fly will distort the hump(s). If anything, this form of indicator is too sensitive. It sounds an alarm when the fly drifts into a strip of fast flow or scrapes the creekbed. As with the bright indicators, the situation dictates which approach is likely to be most effective.

Strike detection is only part one. In part two it is necessary to do something with the signal you have picked up. It's like the difference between receiving a check and getting it cashed. The payoff in tangible returns depends upon part two. Reacting to a signal isn't necessarily an easy thing either. Having worked with many beginners, I can tell you that it is quite typical for the novice to ponder over what he has seen when a flagrant strike sign comes along rather than reacting promptly. He says to himself: "Hey, my leader just jumped backwards 6 inches—by golly, I'll bet a fish is fooling with my fly." A time lapse of two or three seconds in thinking this over is almost always too long. Unlike bass and other fish, trout don't do much chewing after they take. I want to emphasize that tardy response is not an indication of slow reflexes, poor vision, or stupidity. Inability to pull the trigger promptly is perfectly normal at first. Like picking up strike signals, practice is necessary. The ability to set the hook instantaneously and by reflex, even with signals below the level of consciousness, comes with experience. The learner will find that things progress most quickly in settings where there is a lot of positive feedback. By this I mean streams with plenty of willing trout. It's neither educational nor confidence-building when strike signals never come. Even the old pros begin to doubt themselves on these days.

Wet Fly Patterns

Trout probably get a better look at a wet fly than at an artificial up in the surface film. They will hot-iron a wet fly too, so good credibility is essential. Solid takes mean solid signals. Another layer of difficulty has to do with the enormous diversity of underwater food forms. A stream is like an entomologic zoo. In his encyclopedic *Nymphs*, Schwiebert lists 9 separate groups of larvae in addition to freshwater shrimp.[6] When it comes to mayflies, he employs 18 chapters! When you think about creatures that get into the water from the banks, the spectrum of edibles that a wet fly might mimick boggles the mind. Except in select circumstances, hatch matching is impractical. Patterns with general, suggestive appeal are essential. My old reliables are rather plain patterns such as the Gold-ribbed Hare's Ear, Grey Hackle Peacock, and Coachman. The popularity of these venerable flies is neither accidental nor the result of good public relations. Simply, they give an impression of a victual that's worth going after. Although it would be naive to expect a small number of "omni-flies" to suggest creatures as different as an elongate crane fly larva and a stubby mayfly nymph of matronly configuration, you can cover the waterfront surprisingly well with a few effective patterns.

The great old flies that have stood the test of time tend to share certain qualities. For instance a shaggy body outline such as provided by fur dubbing yields a realistic translucency as in the ancient Hare's Ear. If there were a record for the world's fuzziest fly, the Hare's Ear would win, hooks down. It looks like an irritated hedgehog, either that or something swept from under the bed. Materials with surface sheen or reflective qualities such as peacock herl are effective too. The Coachman, Brown Hackle Peacock, and Grey Hackle Peacock are dependable standbys. A bit of tinsel ribbing or a bright spot of color in a wing or tail and hackle fibers that respond to gentle whims of the current are desirable too. With their delicate markings, feathers of the grouse, partridge, and pheasant have appeal. The renowned Wooly Worm proves that functional design is far more important than the way in which a fly is classified. Originally tied as a caterpillar imitation, the ubiquitous Wooly has become

[6]Ernest Schwiebert, *Nymphs* (New York: Winchester Press, 1973), comment not specific to any single page or group of pages.

a general purpose pattern. Of course at times our attention is focused upon a prevalent insect such as the stone fly nymph. Stonies have an elongate wheelbase, and the ones we like to copy are also sizable. Thus, patterns tied on large, long shanked hooks such as the Montana Nymph meet this particular need.

The streamer is a type of wet fly that I find valuable in fishing small water. Many think of the streamer as a river lure, designed to be the undoing of overgrown trout with unwholesome cannibalistic tendencies. Streamers make just as much sense as creek flies, possibly more. Since minnows abound in bankside shoals, close-set banks actually concentrate minnow water. These are meaty flies with the promise of considerable calories for the trout that choose to give chase. And trout aren't shy about taking big bites. I've seen some unbelievable things in varying stages of indigestion that they've swallowed, including a 6-inch watersnake protruding like a cigar from the maw of a 10-inch rainbow. Streamers must be highly visible to the fish, and this is reassuring when the water is high and roily. Whether or not they take the fly, I know it was at least noticed. Streamers are effective during the pre-runoff: sluggish though the trout may be, there is the prospect of garnering a whopping meal in one fell swoop. It's an excellent bargain in energy balance. During the runoff powerful currents batter minnows out of the safety of shoals just as nymphs are torn loose from their burrows and holds. For the same reasons streamers make excellent sense in the rising, roiling water following a heavy rain. I've seen trout attack a streamer with such mass brutality that I was glad to be a large mammal! I try to fish them just as soon as the threat of lethal lightning has passed. Frigid falls bring back conditions like those of the pre-runoff when again the streamer comes into its own. I am particularly fond of white marabou feather for streamer wings. Marabou is fluffy stuff, finely textured and soft as a baby's bottom. The puff of feather becomes a pencil in the water, shimmying and undulating in sensuous fashion even as the tail and fins of a minnow.

By convention streamers are cast more or less across stream, allowed to drift down sideways, and then stripped away from the bank and back toward the angler. I've developed the odd quirk of casting these flies pretty much upstream. For one thing, when the channel is narrow there's hardly room for a cast to the opposite bank with the drift down and strip. For another, a naturally drifting streamer with a pliant wing displays enticing action. The fly tumbles along, the wing going every which way, even out over the eye of the hook like windblown hair. Wing movement is greater during a natural drift than when the streamer is stripped against the current. If the trajectory of the cast is high, the streamer splashes into the water at a steep angle. It will dive and then dart for 6 inches or so before beginning its drift. Instead of scaring the trout silly, this splash-dive-dart sequence sometimes elicits vicious strikes. I've no idea why such a crude presentation should drive the trout up the wall. Perhaps they believe they've found a foolish minnow cavorting near the surface or scurrying in panic from some other predator. You can also season a natural drift by gently twitching a streamer with the rod tip. This little pinch of action is sometimes all it takes.

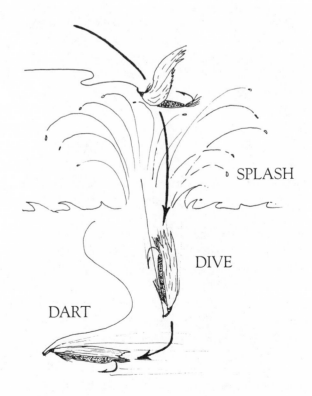

Streamer action on entry.

Fishing Tandem or Multiple Wet Flies

When I was a lad it was common practice to fish a brace of flies or even three artificials on the leader. You could cover more water that way, and it was interesting to see whether the trout would demonstrate a pattern preference. I still like to try these combinations, for example a streamer on the leader's tip and a Hare's Ear as a dropper. When fishing tanglesome creeks, though, I'd stick to a single fly. Targets are so small that you don't need the extra coverage, while the frequency of snags and snarls with two flies is multiplied several times over.

Fly Size

As I have indicated, the very bulk of a streamer gives me a hopeful feeling. However this kind of thinking can also lead to a bad habit. For reasons that I can't defend, for many years I was reluctant to fish dainty wet flies. My fly book contained nothing smaller than a few #12s. It never made sense, since I was perfectly happy to tie on tiny dry flies when indicated. It's dumb to ignore the obvious fact that small adults were once small nymphs and that most aquatic insects are of modest dimension. Insects of a caliber requiring large hooks are really not common during much of the season. Big stone fly and other larvae are more exceptions than the rule. Fishermen are always on the lookout for secrets that might turn a bad day into a good one. The best trick I know is to give small wet flies a try, say a #14, #16, or even a #18. This has worked for me many times, particularly when streams were neither high nor roily, i.e., dry fly conditions sans dry fly action. (When creekbeds are mossy these little wets usually drift right over without snagging, just like a dry fly.)

Weighted Wet Flies

Weighting a fly by adding lead wire to the shank of the hook is a controversial practice. There's an old idea that a fly to which ballast has been added cannot drift or otherwise behave in a natural manner. To many, fly weighting is uncouth. To others, it is as immoral as fishing with bait. For some anglers even thinking about fly weighting is like hearing chalk squeak on a blackboard. The truth is that *appropriate* weighting increases the realism of fly action, and these flies are particularly useful for smaller streams. Weighting a fly is not the same thing as creating a lead sinker armed with a hook and decorated with feathers. Rather, we are talking about the gentle addition of ballast, just a hint of heft. In the case of minnows or larger nymphs such as stone fly or crane fly larvae, you'll find that a weighted artificial approximates the natural more closely than the same fly tied on a naked hook. If you have access to a sensitive analytical balance, you can prove this by collecting food forms such as these and comparing them with weighted and unweighted flies. As naturals grow smaller, so must hook sizes. For flies tied on #14 hooks or smaller, the intrinsic weight of the hook and other tying materials usually is sufficient for a close match.

On the face of things there should be little difficulty in reaching the bottom of small streams, since small presupposes shallow. It turns out to be the other way around. What does it take for a fly cast upstream to sink to the creekbed? Clearly the answer is time. Sink time is strongly influenced by current, and current is in turn modified by what might be called drift span, that is the length of the fly's voyage from its entry into the water to some other point within the target area. You can see that drift span is partially related to target area, larger targets allowing longer drifts. Drift span can also be increased if there is room to cast upstream from the target. We can call this lead space. Although all of these considerations are relative to current velocity, small streams usually severely limit sink time. Targets are almost always small, and the opportunity to lead them isn't there very often. A surfacing rock, protruding bough, or just a sharp bend in the channel will prevent you from putting the fly into a current that feeds the target. This lack of lead space again emphasizes that most creek fishing is done with just the leader and line end in the water. Thus, there is no way for a sinking line to help, whereas a weighted fly will get down quickly on its own. The rock pocket demonstrates the problem of small target size. Because there is little current in the

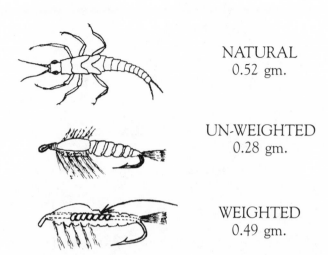

NATURAL
0.52 gm.

UN-WEIGHTED
0.28 gm.

WEIGHTED
0.49 gm.

Weights—natural nymph versus unweighted and weighted artificials.

pocket *per se*, it might seem that a weighted fly would be unnecessary. Not so. The passing tongues of swift flow will catch the leader or line tip within seconds, snatching the fly out of the pocket before it can reach a depth of more than a few inches. By contrast, a weighted fly sinks at once and may be taken by a fish lying at the base of the rock, all within those same few seconds. Or when the trout are plucking food from the passing current face, the highest yield piece of water will be a wedge-shaped area just at the current's very edge where it abuts the slack of the pocket. That wedge is where you'd like your fly to be. If you chuck the fly into the current above the pocket, it's more than likely that it will get carried into the spine of the flow and away from the rock face and that slim wedge of water. A weighted fly lobbed a few inches above the rock and tight to its face enters the water at a steep angle and dives. The brisk current may then suck the lure down farther in the manner of an undertow. This is a deadly presentation. When the water is high, much of the best cover/holding will be found up against the banks. If you have to aim your cast above these bank pockets, leading them, there is much that can go wrong. It's so much easier if you can just peg the fly into the very edge of the money water...much like throwing a dart at the bull's-eye as with a wrist-flick roll cast.

What about crimping a split shot or two onto the leader? Perhaps it's because I wasn't brought up as a bait fisher, but to me split shot is an anathema. Split-shot-loaded leaders are awful things to cast. You get a sort of bolo effect between shot and fly. This matters a great deal when pinpoint presentations are essential. Also, in rapid current the shot will want to bump along the creekbed just where you'd like the fly to be. Meanwhile, your lure rides the current, kite-like, a foot or so above. Worse, a bouncing or drifting shot significantly damps out telltale changes in leader drift that signal a take. Because I depend so much on those signals, crimping on split-shot lessens my effectiveness.

The mechanics of hook weighting may interest tiers. The larger a hook, the more it will weigh, and the more materials it will accommodate. Therefore fly weight is more or less proportional to hook size. If you follow a routine as to the models of hooks you use, the caliber of lead wire, and the quantity of wire applied, you will know about how much a given fly is going to weigh without consulting a scales. I do much of my tying with Mustad models 9671, 9672, and 3906. For #8 hooks and larger I like a medium-diameter lead wire that's about one millimeter in width. For smaller hooks down to #14s I prefer a fine, braided wire that's used for flyline shooting heads. (There isn't room for wire on 16s and 18s, nor would the added ballast be realistic.) Depending upon

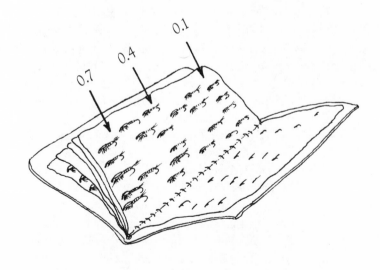

Separating flies by weight.

the pattern and hook, I use between a half dozen and 20 wraps of wire. This gives me a range of weights from 0.15 grams up to about 0.65 grams, and weight corresponds pretty well to hook caliber. My wet fly book is of the wallet type with leather covers and felt leaves. In order to be able to find flies of a particular weight, I stock the center of each leaf with "middleweights" in the 0.4-gram range. Along the right margin go the bantamweights, with the big guys such as stone fly nymphs on #4 hooks on the far left edge. (As a frame of reference, an ordinary paper clip weighs only about 0.5 grams.)

Fly weighting is still another aspect of tackle tuning. During periods of high water, a heavier fly will be needed to reach the creekbed where trout are likely to be holding. When stream levels are low and currents are gentle, a much lighter fly will do the job on the very same stream. For example, let's say you fish a Wooly Worm, size 10. Appropriate fly weights might range from 0.45 grams in early season to an unweighted fly at circa 0.15 grams in the fall. You'll find too that "swum" flies presented across or downstream fish better with a little added weight. In current the fly may surface skip otherwise. This is especially true of streamers with their buoyant wing.

When fishing wet flies on a very short line, the weight of the artificial needs to be kept in mind. Big, heavy flies have so much inertia that they pretty much plow along, resisting drag and pulling the leader behind. However, smaller, lighter flies are going to react to every nudge from the leader, even a gentle lifting of the rod tip. Here longer, finer tippets are very helpful in obtaining a natural drift together with the same techniques used in fishing a dry fly, such as casting slack, lifting line off the water, and so on.

I'm glad to see that more and more tackle shops and catalogs are offering weighted wets. The commercially tied and weighted flies that I have fished have been about right for the hook caliber in question. This trend pleases me because it confirms a long-time bias.

Although I generally put my money on a natural drift, it's an excellent idea to test retrieved or activated flies as well. This is insurance against missing a prevalent, motile food form. The caddis pupa has been the most common explanation for good "swum" fly fishing on small streams in my experience. Caddis pupae are

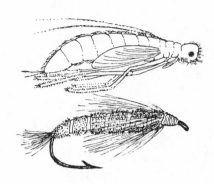

Caddis pupa and imitation.

busy swimmers prior to hatching. A wet fly swung across the current, retrieved against it, or even held static can be deadly. Caddis hatch over a period of weeks, offering spates of both wet fly and dry fly excitement. Certain adult females dive to deposit their eggs on submerged objects, providing further grist for the wet-flyfisher's mill. Still, I believe that a natural drift is the most consistently productive presentation and the safest investment of an angler's time and effort. There's no way to forget the thrill when some subtle message tells of a take and your strike is rewarded by the throb of a trout. For me this is the pinnacle event in all of flyfishing, the point most memorable. The flash of excitement is intense. Learning to present a fly upstream, natural drift takes some determination, commitment, patience, and faith. It's worth the effort! Remember too that the short casts common to small stream fishing bring events in close where learning is easiest.

I've often thought about how fishing would be without wet flies. I'd miss some of the year's best sport, my fishing would end far earlier in the fall, and I'd likely learn to dread heavy summer rains. These are constraints upon my piscatorial life-style that I couldn't accept. I'm never so eager to go astream as in the spring when Nature's whole ambience is in flux. Late season brings solitude, beauty, and the potential for excellent fishing. As for storms, they happen any time they've a mind to. Dodging them is just another thing to worry about, and besides, they usually scramble things in interesting ways. If some oppressive law forced each of us to fish one kind of fly foreverafter, I believe I'd go the wet route. Wets are truly flies for all seasons and all weathers.

7
The Art of Discovery

SIZE

BANK STRUCTURE

CURRENT

ELEVATION

ACCESSIBILITY

Discovering "underfished" and hence semiprivate little streams is a fascinating sub-hobby in and of itself. Maps are essential in finding off-the-beaten-track fisheries. Dry lab sleuthing is also a pleasurable preamble to field explorations. Like a good book, a map can be a facile vehicle for the imagination, making pleasant fantasies easy to come by. If the area is one you've fished before, it's no trick to improve all aspects via a daydream expedition. Larger trout in greater numbers are certain to pursue your flies, perfect weather is assured, and even the scenery becomes more spectacular as you scan the map. If the stream is new, the sky's the limit. Lunkers lurk in virginal pools, and riffles sparkle with trout seldom molested by man. These are the Elysian Fields of an angler's mind. The combination of an up-to-date Forest Service map and a topographic map is ideal. Rather than being repetitious, the two complement one another. Inexpensive Forest Service maps cover large areas. They are updated more frequently than the topographics and are more dependable with reference to man-made structural detail. Clearly, roads and trails are important, as is information about what is and what is not private property. Too often I've explored an apparently remote stream segment, surrounded by what I thought should be national forest, only to find a tightly posted ranch. On the other hand, there is no substitute for the information you get about elevation and terrain contour from a topographic. Understanding the rate of descent of a stream along its different segments is very important in mountainous country. With some practice it's also possible to make educated guesses as to whether the stream runs through a canyon, meanders over meadowy flats, or crosses mixed terrain. Topographics also show detail such as marshes, beaverponds, and springs. There are at least five things about a stream that you can try to surmise:

1. Its probable *size* (width and flow volume).
2. Its average flow rate or *current*.
3. The character of its *banks* (to include vegetation).
4. The altitude or *elevation* of the segment of interest.
5. The relative *accessibility* of the area.

You should get a good idea as to how much fishing pressure a stream is likely to receive as a spinoff. This turns out to be a complex function of the stream's size, bank structure, and accessibility. Finally, these considerations ought to tell you something about the stream's trout population.

Size

At some point every watercourse becomes too small to bother with, even for zealots. The very headwaters of the mightiest rivers begin as runty rivulets, and the trout, too, must have their limits. Quite apart from how the fish view marginal flows, there's the matter of getting your fly into the water in the first place. A gentle, knee-deep flystream with a width of 25 feet or so is the sort that people refer to as "pretty." Wading is easy and even if the creek is willow-flanked, casting shouldn't be too demanding. Farther upstream the width might be cut in half. Now bankside shrubbery threatens to meet over the channel's center. Many inviting pockets are brush bound, and there is little room to maneuver for tricky casts. Fishermen will comment that the creek is becoming "brushy," and many will give up on it. Higher still the flow might dwindle to 6 feet with a complete canopy of boughs and branches. You could perhaps still penetrate this tunnel by duck walking, rod held flat at water level and fanny wet. Fishing now becomes secondary to just getting along. Whether or not the angler continues will be determined by his level of sanity. Had these same banks been carpeted with low green things such as grass, weeds, and flowers as in a wild lawn, the situation would have been different. Sagebrush is also basically friendly. The grey-green shrubs come up to mid-thigh yet seldom interfere with backcasts or overhang enough to shut off casting lanes. So these creeks fish "open." Vegetation is only one aspect of bank structure. There are those steeply canyoned creeks with walls of naked earth or rock that make effective stalking/casting nearly impossible when the water is clear. The twisting, parallel walls force you to try to throw the fly around sharp corners. When you do get close enough to reach the target, it's too close and the trout are spooked.

In guessing at stream size I depend on six variably related observations:

1. Drainage length
2. Drainage area   Related
3. Topography

4. Elevation
5. Average Precipitation   Related
6. Springs

Generally the longer a watercourse, the larger. This is a dangerous estimate basket for too many eggs, though. Some drainages are long and skinny and collect less water than shorter, fan-shaped ones. While it's not necessary to calculate drainage area precisely down to the last square mile with calipers and calculus, a rough estimate will prove helpful. Next consider the topography of the headwaters and upper system. This is a critical facet of surface drainage area. The wrinkled, highly detailed surface of mountainous terrain greatly increases surface area. A topographic map brings out such detail beautifully. A really complex mix of high peaks and deep valleys magnifies the surface area many times over. The impact of wrinkled real estate is a potent one. I think of the majestic Tetons as the outstanding example of how quickly cloud-collecting, vertical summits can spawn watercourses of considerable size and over fairly short drainage distances. The Tetons really don't take up much of the surface of Wyoming/Idaho, yet an awful lot of water pours off their flanks. In mountainous country I tend to incorporate additions from springs into considerations of elevation and precipitation, etc. They can help a timberline brook build muscle quickly. Although trees and shrubs transpire water back into the atmosphere, a heavy canopy holds moisture in the soil and underground water table. Streams passing through heavily forested terrain hold their size better than those traversing sparsely vegetated country.

Latitude is another facet. Anticipating a move to Albuquerque some years ago, I purchased maps for each of New Mexico's national forests. Recognizing that my new state was basically arid, I wanted to learn about whatever trout water might be available. I was pleasantly surprised when I found numerous mountain drainages in the north-central portions of the state. I went a step further by ordering topographic maps to cover the most promising regions, such as the Sangre de Cristo Range and Jemez Mountains near Santa Fe. The Spanish names for these drainages fascinated me. Some, such as the Rio San Antonio, honored saints. Others indicated an association with an animal. I found the Rio del Oso, or River of the Bear, and the euphonious if pastoral Rio de las Vacas, River of the Cows. It was a good lesson about the impact of latitude on stream size, for I found that many of New Mexico's rios would barely qualify as creeks in more northerly states. I suspect that some of them wouldn't be graced with a name at all. They'd just flow on in anonymity. And streams that are of good size on Memorial Day may become ribbons of dust by the Fourth of July. So latitude does count, together with annual rainfall.

After all is said and done there is still no substitute for a passing familiarity with the region in question. If you know what a couple of streams are like for size, it's not difficult to extrapolate using the known drainages as models.

Bank Structure

Although bank structure is difficult to predict from maps, I get some mileage out of three observations:

1. Map symbols or shading that show vegetation patterns.
2. Channel course (relatively straight versus meandering.)
3. Channel cross-sectional contour as shown by lines on a topographic map.

High-detail maps tell you a lot about channel contour. As a rule of thumb, creeks that curve and coil suggest a border of meadowy vegetation rather than dense forest. Map shading may confirm this more directly. Channel profile as seen "on end" is important, too, and is shown by the configuration of contour lines where they cross the stream. If the lines bend into a "V," this is a strong indication of steep, elevated banks if not a true canyon. If the lines cross with no dip or indentation it's likely that the banks will be flat or gently shelving. Canyoned streams are typically brushy. Boulders and dead timber have a way of falling into steep banked creeks, further clogging the watercourse. On a smallish brook deadfall can span from bank to bank, and there is nothing short of a serious-minded barbwire fence (such as the ones around car lots) that is as hard to get over, around, or under as a big old conifer trunk with jagged, gouging limbs. I can think of a dozen little canyons that are crawling with trout where the fish are safe as can be because of deadfall. They make me wish, if only transiently, for a prehensile tail. A fifth extremity such as this would surely prove a bother most of the time, even a source of embarrassment, but think how handy

An open, grassy bank makes a brook that's only a few feet across and fishable.

a tail would be for getting past obstacles in a jackstraw canyon. Perhaps you could even learn to cast with it, thus freeing both hands for scrambling.

Current

Rate of flow is vital. Uniformly swift water in the absence of adequate holding structure is not conducive to a flourishing trout population. Hectic, unremitting current favors neither growth of subsurface vegetation nor an abundance of insect life. Rate of streambed descent over a measured distance translates into average rate of flow. This is easy to figure for any given segment of a stream with the aid of a topographic map. It's an appealing calculation, since flow rate, expressed in feet of descent per mile, is more precise than most of the other features we attempt to guess about. Best of all, you can make some practical generalizations of value from the data. Thus, a stream that drops only 50 feet over the course of a mile is going to be gentle and placid as in a meadow. Double that rate to 100 feet per mile, a nice leisurely pace for a trout stream, and you should find ample detail with pools, riffles, and the like. At 200 feet per mile I'd anticipate swift currents in which holding structure will largely identify the fishable water. At a sustained rate of fall of 400 feet per mile you are going to be dealing with a torrential flow of dubious prospect unless the banks and streambed are dotted with sizable deflectors such as boulders. I begin to write prospective fisheries off my list as flow rates pass the 300 feet per mile mark. Fairly accurate measurements are obtained by looking at the map's scale, counting the crossing lines over an estimated length of stream, and dividing the descent in feet by the measured distance. In nature few watercourses are ruler straight. Still, it's not difficult to visually straighten the segment of interest for your distance estimate. There's no need for a precision cartographer's instrument in making this sort of estimate.

Unfortunately, this simple calculation is not nearly so neat and clean as it sounds. First, the rate at which a stream descends and the amount of water that is coming down are different qualities. Changes in stream level can totally change what the feet per mile figure means to an angler. Creeks that are marginal due to swiftness of flow can still be lots of fun when the water is low. Similarly, the gentlest of streams with an abundance of holding grow white water fangs when levels are high.

Another modifying concept has to do with the uniformity of channel descent along a specific segment of stream. The rate of drop may not be steady throughout. If you had a map that showed the cut-away view of a channel, the streambed might describe a fairly straight line, like a playground slide. However, canyons love to terrace, causing the creekbed to stairstep down. The risers correspond to waterfalls or current chutes, whereas the flats or steps become pools at the foot of each riser. This phenomenon can turn what appears on the map to be a stretch of very swift water into an exciting fishery. Further, the scale of the staircase needn't be particularly coarse in order to create poolets replete with good depth and holding. Sudden drops of a few feet will suffice. Whether or not a topographic will show terracing is determined by the map's scale in comparison with the scale of the watery staircase. When it comes to smaller streams, maps must be highly detailed to show such

tiny wrinkles.

Once in a while a topographic will let you down even when natural detail is coarse enough to be shown by the map's scale. The contour lines suggest a uniform rate of descent when in fact there are steep pitches with relatively slower water above and below. I ran into a Colorado creek that fits this description exactly: The map shows a long meadow ending abruptly where a steep incline in the valley floor is cut by a rapidly climbing canyon. Whereas the meadow has a rate of drop of 120 feet per mile, the canyon above calculates out at an impossible 800 feet. Reaching the meadow's head, I intended to quit until I saw a faint trail along the bank, pitching upward. I followed this rocky path for about a half mile as it grew steeper.

Looking ahead I beheld a nearly vertical jumble of rock faces forming a wall some 300 feet high. My finely detailed map had contour lines in increments of only 40 feet, yet there was no hint of this barrier. Curious, I laboriously picked my way up and over the wall. To my delight I found that it acted as a sort of dam. The creek above became placid again with long, deep currents. The trout were willing, too, and a good deal larger than below. (This is why I hope you'll excuse me for not identifying this stream.) My guess is that this map was prepared stereoptically from offset aerial photos without benefit of ground survey. It may be that the camera didn't see clearly through the heavy screen of conifers along the narrow channel, thus missing the wall and reading a uniform gradient of fall.

We naturally expect to find dwindling diameter as any stream is followed upward toward its ultimate headwaters. This is part of the fun in mapping out a watercourse. You subtract volume and width during an imaginary map trek as each tributary or fork is passed on the way toward the very head. This is a tricky business, though, for you are trading off loss of tributaries against diminished evaporation and ground seepage as you climb, factors that should help sustain volume. Also, incoming rills may be larger or smaller than anticipated. Sometimes a creek loses its stuffing for no apparent reason. Several years ago I was badly fooled by a drainage that I thought held excellent promise. Tributary to a small river, this creek arose in remote, mountain terrain. I knew that the Forest Service had closed an old road that followed the valley some years before and the map showed about 8 miles of water up to the very headwaters. Five miles above the mouth the creek was shown to split into two forks of equal size. Below that point I judged that the width should be adequate, and the rate of descent worked out to a passable 240 feet per mile. The day started well enough. My size estimate was on target, and I quickly caught two fine trout after walking up almost a mile. Things looked good, and yet my crystal ball cracked wide open not 500 yards upstream. Someone or something pulled the plug! The only feeder that I had passed was a pleasant step-across springlet, but suddenly the channel width was cut in half. Worse, the creek that had been knee deep now became a thin, transparent sheet, sluicing down a flat drainboard of cobblestones. The boughs of big spruce were bridging across, too, so I gave up. My five miles of fishable creek had turned into a bare mile. That's how it goes sometimes; you can't win 'em all.

Elevation

Trouting up at timberline is a once-in-a-while, albeit intriguing opportunity for most of us. Part of my evolution as a stream searcher began as a youthful infatuation with the mountains near Denver. In those days, before the smog, you could see a whole string of towering peaks along the western skyline, and among them lay myriad lakes. For me those lonely lakes, nestled in their glacial cirques, held great mystery. I learned that aerial photographs taken by the U.S. Geodetic Survey during World War II could be purchased at the Denver Federal Center. These prints showed the lakes clearly as dark blobs against a textured background of lighter greys corresponding to the chaotic topography of granite basins. It was my goal to find unmapped lakes and streams with the hope that they might contain trout. Timberline terrain draws precipitation like a magnet, so there was a great deal of lake and stream detail. I also found considerable austerity. When I drove my Jeep from the city to 12,000 feet and began to climb on foot, I learned about oxygen deprivation. And I was amazed to see that the seasons other than winter were compressed into about three months. I wondered if summer

really existed at all when I encountered snowstorms in July. At these elevations the water is icy and creeks flow with tremendous velocity due to the vertically disposed glacial terrain. Thus there is a paucity of holding for both the trout and their food forms. Although certain lakes winterkill under a blanket of ice and snow that shuts out sunlight, others contain abundant food. I collected caddis larvae from the shallows at 12,400 feet, watched a heavy hatch of mayflies, and marvelled at the density of freshwater shrimp in a tarn well above timberline. I've seen flights of flying ants and beetles just at treeline and once a swarm of grasshoppers, but by and large the alpine zone is poor pickings for fish in streams.

Beyond this there is the still more fundamental question of whether trout will exist at all in the upper reaches of these skyline drainages. Unlike salmon, they can't get past white-water chutes that are very long or climb high falls. Therefore, unless timberline systems have been stocked, they may well be fishless. This brings a story to mind from the century-old days of the Colorado Gold Rush: While in medical school I was once assigned to the case of a grizzled old miner at the Denver V.A. Hospital. In the process of taking a history I learned that he had spent most of his life working the mines near Breckenridge. My interest took an unprofessional leap when he mentioned the Mayfair Mine in the Ten Mile Range. I knew something of its history. Productive of both gold and silver in the 1880s and '90s, the Mayfair workings lay near the head of Monte Cristo Creek. That name fairly smacked of hidden treasure, and indeed, riches of a finny sort were to be found in Mohawk Lake above the mine's major shafts. We had taken brightly colored, heavily muscled rainbows from the Stygian depths of Mohawk. This 15-acre lake lay at 12,100 feet, poised at the lip of a tundra flat overlooking the valley of the Blue River. Typical of glaciated terrain, it was 400 nearly vertical, ski-jump feet down to the next tundra flat below. Having no other choice, Mohawk's outlet descended in a series of chutes and falls. Eager questions of a nonmedical nature flooded my mind: Did my patient remember this lake? Had it held trout 70 years before, and if so how had they gotten there?

The elderly man seemed to enjoy the memories. "We

had us some dynamite kegs," he smiled. "Strapped 'em to a couple of mules and hauled a few fish up to the top of the tram." I knew what he meant. The tram was a series of rotting timber towers that had supported giant pulleys and metal cables. Buckets were suspended from the cables, and the tram thus carried ore-laden rock from the highest shafts down to a mill on a flat at 11,300 feet. My new friend thought that the trout had come from some beaver ponds that they drained, but remembered clearly "lugging them damn kegs up to the lake." He concluded: "Later, when the fish took hold, we carried up some boards and nailed us a raft." I was enthralled. We had explored much of the old mining operation, camping by its crumbled buildings and poking dangerously into dank, deserted tunnels. I had one more question: There were two other lakes, both quite deep, in the cirque a little higher on Monte Cristo Creek under the very crest of the Ten Mile Range. To our disappointment both were barren so far as we could tell. None of us had ever felt a strike or seen the ring of a rise on their leaden surfaces. What about them?

My query brought a logical response from the ancient miner. He and his fellows had naturally stocked only the closest and most accessible of the three lakes. They were simply establishing a fishing hole for themselves, and one good-sized lake was plenty! The huge tundra basin above Mohawk was drained by a complex of pretty rivulets with a fishy look, most of them just a few feet across. Spongy, green banks were splashed with wildflowers, while the crystalline water gurgled between tiny pools, some as deep as the channel was wide and never touched by fly or worm. It was a place of primal wildness. We occasionally saw black bear and elk while dull-witted ptarmigan waddled about like so many barnyard chickens. But there were no trout. Mohawk had no inlet as such, being fed by springs plus melt from permanent snowbanks clinging to the talus slopes that ringed the lake on three sides. I suppose a few fish got into the brief outlet and literally fell down the falls and chutes that drained into a shallow lake below. It too was barren. With a maximum depth of perhaps 5 feet, this lake froze solid by early winter. So in the extensive drainage of Monte Cristo Creek, Mohawk Lake provided the only fishery.

Another uncertainty involves identifying spawning dates for a particular species over a range of altitude and latitude. No matter that they clog the inlets and outlets, spawning trout can prove a frustration. Their instincts are hardly focused upon feeding. The high country seasonal calendar is so scrambled that it's hard to predict spawning dates, and a miscalculation can ruin a whole trip. That happened to us once during August at Mohawk Lake. Rainbows are customarily spring spawners, yet the only fish we caught were males that virtually dribbled milt. We wondered what time of season August 10th might be? Surely not spring and yet not quite fall either, even above 12,000 feet.

When lakes do have inlets and outlets, the prespawning period is sometimes dynamite. During a discussion with a newcomer from Michigan, I remarked that the Southwest offers better fishing than many suppose for smallish trout. I detected a note of skepticism when he replied: "I've only been out once since I got here and I guess I was pretty lucky." Pressed for details, he indicated that the previous fall he had driven up to Platoro Reservoir at the head of the Conejos River in southern Colorado, returning with a 23-inch brown! I agreed that there were indeed some sizable trout in our lakes, only to learn that this trophy had come from the tiny Adams Fork above the reservoir. Hiking along the shore, he saw the creek and walked up a little way, casting casually, nothing to it. No doubt that huge fish had entered the small stream to spawn later in the fall, a well-recognized phenomenon.

Accessibility

When conditions are just right, small headwaters streams can hold large trout without the assistance of a nearby lake. The family of a college friend had a cabin on the Blue River near Dillon, Colorado, back in the days when Vail was nothing but a cow pasture. A whole series of creeks spill off the Gore Range and into the Blue River on the eastern side. Although most of these drainages have one or several lakes in their high basins, according to maps the stream closest to the cabin was an exception. In hopes that this was an error, Don and his brother decided to explore its upper reaches. They managed to catch a few rainbow-cutthroat hybrids before the trail petered out altogether and found themselves in a devil's landscape of jagged, rocky outcroppings punctuated by deadfalls of huge conifer. As boys will, they pushed on, climbing ever higher through this howling wilderness. They passed a cougar sitting atop a boulder that watched them with seeming boredom and finally reached timberline at the foot of a brief meadow. Snugged up against the talus slope below the final summit of the Gore Range, the creek had become a standing broad jump. Still, it had depth and undercut banks. Re-rigging their rods, the boys hoped to catch some small cutthroat. They were half right. Don's fly got swallowed on the first cast by something that carried it under a bank and summarily broke his leader. And so it went. That half mile's worth of meadow was a stronghold for exceptionally fat, native cutthroat, most of them pushing 18 inches and flirting with 2 pounds. They were able to land only a few of the fish they hooked, but it was a day to remember. That tiny meadow constituted a fragile fishery, one that could never withstand much pressure. Those miles of nearly impassable, tortured terrain were the only reason it existed at all. The meadowy flatness of that last stretch of creek under the talus slope was essential too; otherwise there would have been insufficient holding and food content to support such splendid specimens. Those cutthroat must also have grown better than they spawned, else there would have been a crowded population of stunted fish as is so common with brook trout.

If there is a unifying formula for success in ferreting out small streams, it includes keeping an open mind as to where sport might be found combined with a positive attitude and reasonably adventuresome spirit. The very best trout trackers I've met share a good measure of the "four I's." These are inquisitiveness, imagination, intuition, and ingenuity. And when you've gone to a lot of trouble to get at a sure bet that turns out to be fishless, a fifth "I" can be added: Insanity!

8

Where Other Anglers Aren't

Where Other Anglers Aren't

By nature flyfishing tends to be a reflective, private pastime. For the small stream fisherman, finding a degree of solitude is more than personal preference. Whereas rivers accommodate large numbers of sportsmen without undue friction, there's real trouble when anglers queue up along a creek. The fishing can be ruined for everyone. This is why it's sensible to try to predict where competitors will be (and not be) through the application of a little insight into human nature plus some applied psychology.

There is an oft-repeated and tiresome canard to the effect that modern Americans are lazy. How often have you heard the fable that after hiking one mile you'll be alone? Nonetheless, the outdoor public comes in all shapes and sizes, from remarkably preserved elderly folk to newborn babies strapped into papoose packs. Family dogs count, too. Young and old, four-legged and two, it's a mixed bag. However, the purposes for which people are out and about are less varied. Many are seeking a wilderness experience. The happy wanderers or lederhosen-clad backpackers are intent on covering a certain length of trail between dawn and dark. The jut-jawed, bearded macho types toting ropes and pitons are out to scale some summit. Disciples of Thoreau are into birds and bees, shrubs and trees. None of the members of these subgroups is liable to disturb an angler along the stream. Hikers rarely do more than dabble or bathe in brooks, sometimes (regrettably) doing their laundry. The survivors and climbers look down on us effete flyrod types with disdain. And on several occasions I've been the target of snide remarks from "naturalists" who apparently regarded my activities as heinous. For that matter, there is little competition from anglers bound for the high lakes. Inaccessible though they may be, lakes have tremendous magnetism. A standing body of water will lure all sorts of visitors whose commitment to fishing is otherwise marginal. Although trails commonly follow creeks up to the lakes that they drain, streams are seldom bothered by anglers who are "lake-bit."

The camper-trailer crowd constitutes another major group that contrasts with the wilderness types. They will have brought as many of the comforts of home along as possible. Their umbilical cords connect them to the gasoline motor; lawn chairs lashed atop mobile homes between television antennae. There are indeed fishermen among them, but I'd not expect to meet a member of this clan along a brushy creek.

Then there are those to whom the lure of freshly stocked rainbow is irresistible. For them the stocker truck is a pied piper, and the "put-put" of its air compressor a song of promise. Once during a heavy runoff I was working the outlet of a lake hard by a highway when I heard that tell-tale signal off in the distance. The sound grew nearer, interrupting the sunny serenity of the afternoon. The fish truck pulled off onto a dirt road and stopped along the bank on the far side. I watched a uniformed Fish and Game official get out and take a long-handled dip net from the back. Within a matter of seconds a sedan careened off the blacktop, dust flying, and skidded to a halt by the truck. I went back to my fishing until I was distracted by the sound of angry voices some time later. A crowd of people gathered around the truck were engaged in agitated discussion. That evening when I stopped for gas at a store where the dirt road joins the highway, I asked the owner if he knew anything about the commotion. "Just some yay-hoo," he replied. "Got his monofilament tangled around the aerial of the fish truck." "Dave (whom I presumed to be the F & G man) was mad as hell."

Since almost all stocking is done at points of easy access to water from a road, such spots receive inordinate pressure. I personally avoid these places. With their fins rubbed down to nubbins against the walls of hatchery tanks, these stocker rainbow (or Venus De Milo trout) offer little challenge. Obviously, I have nothing against any of these neighbors. They just hear a different drummer. It's likely a good thing too. Taken together, these are the major outdoor folk forms. Remaining are a few exceptions to the rules plus a small cadre of addicts such as myself.

Seduction by the Waters

Assuming that it is possible to refine our list of outdoor types and to identify the real competitors, let's look at some very basic principles of angling psychology. One of the most common is a human failing in which I share. It might be called "seduction by the waters." To paraphrase, it is very difficult to walk or even to drive by good-looking water without stopping to fish. And, as we all know, once you get into a stream there's an excellent chance of spending the rest of the day nearby. Thus, this phenomenon tends to protect the more remote portions of drainages without necessarily being related to laziness or sloth on the part of other anglers. This is truly a powerful form of seduction, too. Pretty water issues a compelling invitation, a visual siren call. Although the angler's fate, should he succumb, is not so dire as that of the sailors in the Odyssey, the best fishing is rarely found in the first sexy water we come

to close upon a trail head, parking area, or bridge. It's a safe bet that streams will be hardest hit close to points of access.

Beyond this consideration, some streams fish faster than others. It's easy to race by long stretches of swift, flat water lacking in distinctive character. If the lower stretches of a creek are of this nature, fishermen will scatter readily upstream. Conversely, a segment with a nice set of staggered pools can be expected to greatly slow upstream migration.

Another aspect involves the physical characteristics of a stream. If a brook with four fishable miles of water is fairly straight of channel, open of bank, and followed by a good trail, the average visitor might cover most of its length in a day. Decorate those banks with dense thickets, take away the trail, twist the channel into kinks, and you have a very different proposition. The Box Canyon of the Brazos River in northern New Mexico is a perfect example of how difficult going influences fishing pressure. On its own scale this canyon is as spectacular and awesome as any geological phenomenon I've seen. Sheer walls of granite rise 500 feet on either side. Occasional pines lean out over the crevasse from crannies in cliff faces, outlined against a thin, twisting ribbon of blue sky. Box canyons are so named because of close-set and very steep sides that turn at sharp angles. This creates the illusion that the stream is issuing directly from the base of a rock face up ahead while equally sheer walls close in to the left, right, and behind. Box canyons are not for claustrophobics! The Brazos has no real trail thanks to a litter of deadfall from the rims interposed among a menagerie of boulders. The combination of an impassible cliff face plus deep, swift water forces the visitor to ford repeatedly. It's slow going because there's no way to maintain a steady pace what with boulders to clamber over or squeeze between, tree limbs to walk, and fordings. Approximately a mile from the mouth you come to a dramatic 25-foot waterfall known as the "first falls." With the exception of individuals fresh out of Marine boot camp, it takes most people about an hour to reach this landmark. Getting around the first falls involves a scramble past a 45-degree slope composed of loose, perfidious shale. Then three-quarters of a mile farther lies the double-tiered second falls. This barrier is still tougher. It's dank and gloomy

Claustrophobic box canyons contain lots of trout but few fishermen.

but only after they've resisted the huge pool and accepted the task of negotiating the steep slope to get around the cataract. Proving the point, the amount of trash below the falls is probably ten times that found just above where there is very little people sign. The quality of fishing below the barrier is sufficient to satisfy most anglers anyway. Knowing all this, when we set out there is mutual agreement that there will be no stopping for any reason short of fracture until the first falls is behind us. No exceptions! We find it safer not to rig up at the mouth either. Being on the ready is a sore temptation when passing the tail of a pool disturbed by rising rainbow. The 75 minutes so invested are likely well spent, for the quality of action jumps a full quantum on the upstream side of the cascade.

The Brazos Box is an extreme example of pressure concentration near the accessible end of a strip of stream. Few fisheries are so rugged or show such a sharp fall-off in competition over so short a linear distance. Nonetheless, the principle is dependably sound. I've long practiced a watered-down version of our Brazos Box strategy in trail fishing ordinary streams. I call it my 25-minute rule. I put my head down and walk for most of a half hour away from the point of access before starting to fish. Why 25 minutes? There are two reasons: First, I've found that most people can't wait through more than 15 minutes worth of walking, giving me a 10-minute edge. Secondly, I can't control my own impulses beyond about 25 minutes.

Ugly Duckling Phenomenon

Next we come to the dilutional factor, or the observation that a concentration of good fishing water, streams or lakes, will spread out the pressure. If all of the various fisheries have about the same degree of angler appeal, the distribution of pressure may be fairly even. Otherwise, the less attractive fisheries can be nearly virginal, a sort of ugly duckling phenomenon. This can be seen when there are only two or three fishable waters in close proximity if one is more noticeable than the other(s). Take a pretty lake fed by a bashful brook, or a famed river and its timid tributary. Overshadowed, the lesser water often receives surprisingly

in the shadow-splashed box save at midday, and the old adage about what goes up, must come down, creeps into the mind as you penetrate ever deeper. Getting out is just as tedious, and this is no place to be at nightfall. Prospects of spraining an ankle or breaking a leg are good enough by day.

The first half mile is a series of deep pools. These beckon the bait fishers in particular, as attested by worm cartons strewn about. A gargantuan pool graces the foot of the first falls, all foam flecked and shrouded in mist. The falls clearly stops most anglers. It's like a closed gate between them and the water above. The gate will open, little notice, perhaps far less than its merit deserves. Some of these secondary waters might attract a fair amount of attention if they existed alone, out of the shadow of their showier sisters.

"Out of sight, out of mind" is another important principle. I apply this phrase to relatively accessible segments of streams that get skipped over because they are less than plainly evident. For example, the creek that runs away and hides from a road that has been hounding it, temporarily scurrying behind a ridge or into a canyon. Although it's not necessarily difficult to get at such water, many anglers ignore these shielded stretches. This is a rather common occurrence. An example: The Roaring Fork River upstream from Aspen is fairly small. Approaching from the east down Independence Pass with Aspen just ahead, the canyon floor suddenly falls away, leaving the highway clinging to the mountainside to descend in a series of timid switchbacks. There, tilting onto its nose, the Roaring Fork truly begins to roar as it spills into a long, granite-walled chute. You can see it far below, a churning ribbon of white. Then a dense screen of aspens shields the valley floor from further view until after a few miles a gap in the green wall reveals the Roaring Fork again, meandering placidly not far below the shoulder of the highway. There's just one problem. The river is now on posted private property. As you anticipate, there is reason to wonder what the stream is like between the base of the white water chute and the quiet meanders. Again the combination of a Forest Service map plus an accurate topographic map gives that information. The bottom or downstream end of the chute is shown nicely by the topo, whereas the private property stands out as a rectangle of white against the green of National Forest land. There is just over a mile of legally fishable river with an average rate of drop of 170 feet/mile between the bottom of the chute and the fence line. The fishing? Follow a deer trail down from the highway some day and give it a try. I predict you won't see anyone else even though it's just a 15-minute drive from town.

Posting

Determining which pieces of a stream are open and which are posted can become a major problem in an unfamiliar area. Sorting out fence lines, gates, roads, and signs is frustrating and also a waste of fishing time. More than once I've used up much of a day and most of a tank of gas in the process of scouting things out. It's also unsettling to get run off when you've no idea you were trespassing in the first place. This can happen in situations where there is no posting or warning. Local lore is often helpful, but how is a newcomer to know these things? "The three miles of Beaver Creek below Old Man Johnson's barn and down to the county bridge are on his place and he don't let nobody in"—that sort of thing. Getting tossed out can be scary too. I was once asked to absent myself, post haste, from Michigan Creek near Fairplay, Colorado, by a man who very pointedly unfastened the holster flap of a big revolver. True enough, he did show me a sign on the way out, no matter that it was small, weathered beyond readability, and bent almost flat to the ground! All this near "Fairplay"? My most trying experience took place in Wyoming during an attempt to get into the lower reaches of a tributary of the North Platte River. Firmly believing this to be Bureau of Land Management terrain, I set forth in my trusty truck. It took a good hour to reach my destination, where dim tracks faded into a grassy swale leading down to the creek a half mile beyond. On the way I had passed through three fences with gates, two of them open and the third unlocked. At no time had I seen any sign or form of printed communication, whether friendly, hostile, or noncommittal. Aside from a couple of deserted mine shafts, those roads and fences were the only evidence of human habitation. The brook turned out to be a bit wider and deeper than anticipated. It was seasoned with bouncing riffles such that my fingers trembled as I threaded the rod. About then I became aware of an odd aroma. Cigar smoke! Why here? Turning, I beheld a smallish man puffing a largish stogie and eyeing me in a way I intuitively found unfriendly. Bidding him a polite good morning I suggested that, to our mutual benefit, I would be happy to pursue a course, upstream or down, so as not to conflict with his fishing. (He carried a spinning rod with wormed bait hooks.) Sliding the cigar to the corner of his mouth, the man replied in Texanese that he would indeed like to see me pursue such a course, namely "the hell out of here." Pointing to a small shack on the far bank hidden in the willows, my host stated that he owned much of the valley, both sides, and went on to ask whether I realized that I had committed trespass on a very famous ranch enroute to my parking place? And was I aware that those same roads were regularly patrolled by his friends, the ranch hands who, by the way, were duly deputized by the local sheriff? He further assured me that they would be only too glad to bring me before the local magistrate. (I assumed at gunpoint, possibly lashed to the hood of a pickup.) This made me angry. I questioned the legality of such punitive action, given the total and complete absence of any sort of warning, notification, or even dim suggestion of private property status. His countenance grew even colder, and biting tatters from the cigar's butt (which he spat into the water) he replied plainly enough: "People are supposed to know." What to do? It would be enormously satisfying to ask for proof of ownership and I noted the absence of any visible form of weapon. On the other hand I glimpsed the glint of a vehicle's bumper parked behind the shack. I had visions of a B movie plot: Powerful, corrupt rancher with local lawman in pocket bullies innocent homesteader. Anyway, given the existing odds and potential penalties, I wasn't persuaded to call the Texan's bluff or to play the hero's role this time around. So back up the swale I went, tail between legs and rod at half mast. Was I a coward?

Posting isn't invariably a bad thing though. A thoughtful and resourceful angler can sometimes use private property to his advantage. The act of poaching must be as old as the concept of private property, but I'm not talking about *that* ancient art. As noted, ambiguous situations in which it's hard to tell where private property begins or ends are not infrequent. Thus water that appears to be verboten may in fact be fair game. Therein lies the secret, for I've found that the fishing public tends to look at these things rather superficially. Let's use another of my favorite Wyoming fisheries as a case in point: Picture a huge, open valley with a nice stream bridged by a state highway. To the

west of the bridge lies a beautiful ranch with scores of fat Herefords grazing contentedly in expansive pastures. This is a manicured, businesslike, no-nonsense operation. So are the signs. You know what I mean: "Prosecuted to the fullest extent," etc. Fittingly, the fence on the side where the buildings stand is tall, tight of wire, and barbed. It happens that an identical fence separates the road from very similar pastures on the east side. These also contain fat Herefords, but there is one big difference. That fence isn't signed. The thing is it ducks into and out of clumps of willows so you really have to pull off, park, and walk the fence to be sure. It appears that the big ranch has posted both sides of the bridge when in reality the water to the east is public domain. Despite being a very pretty flystream, competing anglers are few. If the state were to put in a stile and a sign saying "Fisherman Parking," I'd bet pressure would increase many times over. The nearest town is 25 miles away, and I doubt that many visitors think to ask about this creek.

Another phenomenon that's worth recognizing is *barrier property.* In the process of working up or down a stream you come to a fence that says "NO." If the extent of the barrier property is unknown either as to its length along the channel or its width along the banks, you'll have to make a decision. There are three choices: You can walk around, turn back, or trespass. Assuming you do decide to walk the line to its far side, will there be adjacent, contiguous property that's also posted? Given this dilemma, many anglers just quit. Sometimes that's wise, but what if the barrier property is small with public water just beyond? Obviously, that's just what you'd like to find, and pressure on the far side could be much reduced. I'm always on the lookout for sandwiched segments of public water between posted properties. These can be outstanding. My favorite is a mile's worth of stream in the Colorado San Juans. (A sense of loyalty precludes further identification since this was an entrusted secret.) By the highway there is a major Forest Service campground with a road that continues for about a half mile. There the tracks are stopped dead by a posted gate. The accompanying fence goes right down into the water, resuming on the far side and climbing a steep bluff face. This big ranch is curiously split into halves separated in the middle by a mile of

Forest Service land. You ford at the lower fence, follow it up the bluff perpendicular to the stream, and then walk the level bluff for a mile until the fence line heads back to the bank. I estimate that fewer than 5 percent of the people in the campground know this, and they don't let on. Would you?

Asking Permission

The best of all possible solutions is being permitted to fish. It can't hurt to ask. Although I've no trade secrets, there are some common sense dos and don'ts. For instance, don't show that you're in a rude rush to get at the stream even though you slaver to do just that. This means avoiding skidding to a halt in the ranch yard, dust flying and livestock scattering. It means not slamming car doors or sprinting, rod in hand, to pound on the rancher's door as if his barn were on fire. Park quietly at a discreet distance and then just amble on up to the porch. If anyone's home, by all means stop and chat a spell before popping the question. Whereas us city types get tired of people and their incessant chatter, country folk can be lonely. Like everyone else, they have natural curiosity, in this instance about you. Neither do they like to be taken advantage of. If a rancher permits you to rummage about his place, taking fish out of his creek, possibly leaving trash behind or gates open, what's in it for him? Small talk is truly an art, and it's also a courtesy. The real experts I've fished with make the request for trespass privileges sound like an afterthought. It seems as if they had really dropped by for a visit and, discovering by chance that they have some tackle along, wonder if it might be okay to see how they're biting? I also know one entrepreneur who carries a small supply of gift bottles of whiskey in the trunk of his car against the need. This is a level of finesse beyond my scope, but after all, a rancher's liver is his own affair. To conclude, it's well to remember that many country folk look on flyfishers (as opposed to bait fishers) as odd and queer. To them you will constitute a curiosity. I shall never forget a grizzled old fellow who invited me into his cabin to "see somethin' special." I was very glad to accept the offer, for it prevented his dog from continuing attempts to amputate one of my lower extremities. There in a side room stood a spanking new, green-marbled toilet with shiny flush handle, seat and lid, the whole works. This convenience was clearly as yet unused, since it sat propped up on two-by-fours on a dirt floor. Like a throne it was. After admiring this gleaming fixture I went on to express an interest in trying my feathered hooks on the sinuous creek winding through the front pasture. I could sense he thought me peculiar. For my part I couldn't help but notice that his cabin had no indoor water source!

I've described various strategies to help one avoid his fellow man along the stream as if each were distinct and separate. In real life these phenomena commonly occur in clusters. I often fish a stream that incorporates at least four of these features into one package: Coming off a high plateau it wanders through an expansive meadow where it has been dammed to form a reservoir. It's a scenic spot with a popular campground, and just below the dam the stream oxbows through another mile of really gorgeous water. Then abruptly the channel straightens against the face of a mountain, becoming swift and canyoned for the next mile and a half. Emerging, the creek winds through still another pretty meadow, which leads it to a bridge on the highway. That lower meadow is tightly posted. While you can see the canyon from the highway, there's no way to tell where the posting ends. Approaching the canyon from the reservoir requires walking through that seductive meadow while the canyon *per se* is not especially inviting. Both banks are very steep and heavily overgrown by thick-trunked alders interspersed with conifer. Instead of following the water, the dim trail is cut high along the mountainside. Thus, the private property at the lower end protects the canyon from that side, while the nifty meadow water seduces many would-be visitors from the other. Whereas the reservoir is stocked regularly, the canyon has probably never been planted, and finally, the canyon is a relative ugly duckling, too. The truth of the matter is that the canyon is on Forest Service land, seldom gets fished, and is correspondingly full of fat "brownies"!

I have neglected the most obvious people-avoidance maneuver of all. Competition is sure to be far greater on Saturdays and Sundays than during the week. In my observation the magnitude of this difference can be as much as 10 to 1. Therefore, when you can afford the luxury of a weekday excursion, take advantage by all means. Otherwise, tactics designed to buy you relative aloneness are especially important on holidays and weekends. The seasonal waxing and waning of angling pressure is also worth remembering. The traffic jam occurs during the spring, fading as midsummer passes until you'll have the water almost to yourself when those pleasant fall days arrive. Part of this has to do with the understandable urge to get out again after a long winter. Early birds are a tough and dedicated lot. You'll see them in clusters, wading crotch-deep in icy snowmelt midst the blasts of a spring blizzard. Another attraction is the high, discolored water of early season. This gives bait and lure fishers cover for their heavy tackle and water enough to fish it. For both reasons I avoid weekend outings in the early spring.

When you do hit streams in the winter and spring it's always a good plan to try the lower ends of drainages that may have been marginal fisheries during the summer due to low water levels and high stream temperatures. Browns in particular are prone to extend their range downstream in winter. A local stream shows about 8 miles worth of elasticity in this regard. Most everyone becomes accustomed to driving by the foothills portions during the hot months, yet when the banks are snowy some of the largest trout of the entire season are taken from this lonely segment.

There are several other tricks that I have found helpful in avoiding conflicts with other anglers. It is sometimes a good ploy to walk downstream past the water you intend to fish back through. If there's a trail and the stream is visible you will learn whether there are competitors. If so you can probably tell if they are working upstream or down. So often the other person will be fishing bait or lures downstream. This really isn't much of a problem for a flyfisher headed the opposite way. Anglers traveling in opposite directions put a lot of channel between themselves pretty quickly.

This brings up the question of how long it takes trout to settle down and become catchable again. I've heard optimistic estimates of as little as ten minutes and contrastingly gloomy prophesies of "all day." There can be no single answer because so many factors come into play. Stream-size is one. A river in all of its capacious

parts is less disturbed by a passing angler than is the intimate anatomy of a brook. Obviously, fishermen casting from the bank create less havoc among the finny folk than do wading anglers, while partisans of pools who skip everything in between leave whole strips of stream virginal. Finally, it seems that in any case a good hatch will quickly restore the trout's confidence and cupidity.

Tracking

The worst calamity of all is to get close behind another angler without knowing it. This can mean a skunking for the trailing fisherman. It's the stuff nightmares are made of. This sort of mishap can sometimes be avoided if you are a proficient tracker, Indian style. Wet marks on rocks are reasonably obvious signs of nearby competition. (Don't be fooled by splash spots made by capricious little currents that spout sporadically.) You may see a sandprint on a rock, perhaps dry, yet with grains still rolling off the convexity. Also, as all Boy Scouts know, sharp-edged, distinct prints in mud or sand are fresh, particularly if the edges are crumbling. Crushed or bent down grass or weeds, still in the process of straightening, mean that someone is just ahead, and so do transient spates of roil. Sometimes it's only a cow, but those little passing clouds of murk indicate that something's afoot. Wildlife can serve as an ally too. Squirrels chatter and scold, bawdy jays squawk, and nesting robins curse. These creatures are very dependable about announcing the presence of others, whether ahead or coming from behind. A cobweb strung across the throat of a tiny target is a special intimacy of small streams and a reassurance. Where there are webs, no one else has fished that day.

Leapfrogging

All of this talk about avoidance suggests that flyfishers are basically antisocial. Nothing could be further from the truth. We are a remarkably gregarious lot. Birds of a feather, we flock to teach each other how to tie flies, how to cast them, and we love to sit through each other's slide shows, the ultimate test of communal feeling. Still, there is the question of *where* to be friendly. What about a small trout stream? There are several advantages to sharing streamside experiences. It is fun to anticipate the excitement of a trip during the planning stages and to compare notes after it's over. There are also benefits of congeniality through cooperative experimentation. It's important to identify the sort of water that is most productive and the presentation that is most effective. The same holds for the type of fly, size, and pattern. You may have a pretty good idea about how things are likely to go beforehand, but considerable adjustment is still accomplished on site.

The objections to fishing small streams in tandem are obvious. Apart from getting in one another's way, tangling lines and all that, there is the real threat of spooking each other's water. "Leapfrogging," or taking turns in leading the way up the stream, is the usual solution. Leapfrogging is almost an art, for a great deal of mutual coordination and cooperation are required. There's more to this than just alternating positions, turn-about's-fair-play. Given that reworking freshly fished water is seldom a rewarding experience, an equitable means of changing the guard, leader and follower, is necessary. When the trailing partner passes his friend to become the new leader, said friend will need to be alerted to the fact and will need to see where his buddy enters the stream above. Otherwise the new trailer can't know when he has entered "used" water.

If this is going to work, the fishing pace of the two partners will have to be similar. Things don't go well when one partner is more competitive than the other or simply fishes faster. If a tortoise and a hare get paired off, the poor tortoise is in for a bad experience. He's not going to get in his fair share of time as leader because of lengthy trips through the thick and thorny in pursuit of his projectile partner. I've had lots of practice as a tortoise, since boys are apt not to fish as slowly and carefully as their fathers. Boys are highly prone to succumb to the lure of greener grass—the stream just ahead always looks especially fishy. The easiest leapfrogging is along grassy, meadow streams with open banks and lots of tight meanders. Just a few steps along the bank, cutting across several knuckles, buys a lot of creek length, and visual contact is not a problem. My buddy Charlie from Sheridan, Wyoming, is the smoothest fellow I've ever fished with. Charlie is a notably loud, off-key whistler and audible over the noise of currents. Charlie claims that moose are offended by his music along the willow-packed meadows of the Tongue River in the Bighorns. (A cow moose with a calf in tow is not a healthy companion midst the maze of a willow thicket.) Then Charlie's ever-present cigar helps too, both in locating his position and in further offending any nearby moose or bear. Although fishing tandem is an excellent way to practice angler tracking, I'm afraid that under the best of circumstances leapfrogging wastes a certain amount of good water. Coming up to the bank at right angles, I chronically find myself right on top of a prime target that I've likely spooked. As to three-angler leapfrogging, forget it. Instead of being additive, the difficulties are raised to the third power!

9
Beaverponding

Beaverponds offer a change of pace on small streams. Indeed at times beaver work their magic on springs and rills so small that no fishery would exist at all were it not for their efforts. I think of these ponds as "can be" opportunities. They can be this way or that. Many are as small as backyard swimming pools. Others are large enough to qualify as lakes. Certain ponds crawl with trout while others are barren. If there are fish and the pond contains good supplies of food, trout display explosive growth. Alternatively, lesser food content plus an opportunity to spawn leads to a crowded population of stunted trout. Ponds may be startlingly transparent or murky, deep or shallow, and so on. Even a specific pond won't hold still for you. Picture a glassy surface with trout rising well out from the bank. Getting a fly to those fish without spooking them is no mean task, and once frightened, trout spread panic throughout the entire pond. But let a gentle breeze spring up or a misting shower riffle the surface, and the challenge virtually disappears.

Finding Ponds

It is difficult to predict just where these ponds will be found, because beavers don't need much of a flow to work with. Like the Army Corps of Engineers, beaver have an insatiable need to build dams. I've been told that the mere sound of running water is enough to trigger their urge to chop, trim, and stack. A friend who runs a resort was having trouble with several of these creatures (beaver, not engineers) who persisted in damming the tiny inlets to his stock ponds. He claims that a naturalist advised him to place some device that would buzz or make a whirring noise such as a battery-powered electric razor in a nearby dry ravine. The waterlike sound was supposed to encourage the beaver to build their dams there. Do you buy that story? In any case, the beaver can do a lot with minimum flows. In-out exchange will have to be sufficient to keep the water fresh if the pond is to sustain trout, although a mere spring may suffice. Such springs are not necessarily going to show on maps or cut any sort of canyon for themselves. Springs even enter through pond beds, while outflow may be a matter of seepage and evaporation. Beaver can back up a stream of surprising size when an abundance of building materials is at paw and tooth. However, these ambitious structures don't generally withstand the ravages of the runoff or summer cloudbursts for very long.

Another pattern of ponds might be likened to a string of pearls along the course of a small stream or large spring. Such ponds are usually quite small and close-set, each dam being built across the outflow of the pond just above. Tiny pondlets such as these often escape the cartographer's attention. Then there are ponds and whole pond systems that the beavers desert for reasons best known to themselves. This means that the ponds will soon drain down to mud puddles, for the dams require constant repair and renovation by their chisel-toothed landlords.

Trout Populations

If you do come upon a group of ponds, there is no assurance that they will hold fish. Beaverponds are good bets to winter kill and can die of old age, too. Decaying water weed and other vegetable matter provide a rich source of nitrogen and function as natural fertilizer. It's a kind of aqueous compost for the pond's flora and fauna. Eventually there can be too much fertilization. The water becomes relatively acid and inhospitable to trout, insects, and even to plant life. Only a special form of greenish-blue algae remains. This is why younger ponds are said to be better bets than ancient ones. I once discovered a prehistoric monster of a pond on the floor of the Blue River Valley in Colorado. My curiosity was aroused by a peculiar strip of high, grassy bank capped by immense willows. Beyond the willow fringe there were no trees as far as I could see until the canyon wall began to climb a good half mile away. I forded, climbed the steep, soggy slope, and wedged my way through the wall of packed willows. Parting the last fronds, I was startled to see fully 10 acres of fishy-looking lake glistening in the sun. It was an otherworldly place. The pond was fringed by poisonous water hemlock, tall, long-stalked plants with umbrella caps of white flowers. And weren't those surface rises? Elongate shadows scudded between clumps of water weed as I excitedly worked out line, placing my fly to intersect the path of an approaching fish. The creature took no notice of my lure, continuing toward me, and I wondered if I could make a second cast without frightening my quarry. Then I realized that I had been one class off in my taxonomy. The "fish" had an ugly, toad-like head and external gills! These were salamanders of course, waterdogs, and the rises I had seen were merely bubbles of gas coming off a thick layer of sun-warmed, rotting debris on the bottom. I should have figured this out beforehand, since there was hardly a way for trout from the river to climb

the high embankment. Meanwhile, the giant pond was fed by tiny springs coming down the canyon wall, and it drained through seepage into the river with no outlet as such.

Disappointing though the ancient lake turned out to be, it provided momentary excitement. It's that way with a hidden pond when you chance upon one — like finding a treasure box, mysterious of content. Perhaps it will be devoid of fish, but given the right conditions, beaverpond trout can grow to phenomenal size. I've seen impressive cutthroats and rainbows taken from them and a brown that strained credulity. It was a hook-jawed monster, heaved unceremoniously via pitchfork from a small pond that was being drained near Laramie, Wyoming. Even the colorful brookies, so often overpopulated and stunted, can grow to large size in this setting.

Ponds that do hold large trout may change rapidly. I've studied a picturesque beaverpond fishery that's cut into the side of a high plateau in the Colorado San Juans. The plateau catches water that feeds myriad springs, trickling down to an aspen-strewn bench, an idyllic setting for beaver. Accordingly, they built a veritable city of dams, ponds, and houses consisting of some three dozen little lakes up to about 5 acres in surface area. I don't know the early history of that bench, however in the mid-1960s the larger ponds held some truly magnificent brookies weighing as much as 3 pounds! By 1971 the fishing was still excellent, but only from the standpoint of numbers of fish to be caught. The average brookie went about 8 inches.

They would rise to pine cones and even apple cores like trained dolphins. Then in 1978 every pond we tested was barren aside from frogs and waterdogs. I felt sad, for the stagnating ponds were murky and shrunken, the place smelled swampy, and the beaver were gone. There was a pervasive sense of decay.

Reading Ponds

There's no need to read a pond when the surface area is small. You can cover much of the water with a few casts. When there are surface rises, there's no problem either. Otherwise I miss the detail that helps me read a stream. It can be a frustrating puzzle to know where to put your fly on a large beaverpond. I try to get maximum mileage out of stream-reading principles. For example, I watch the water just off the bank very carefully. Many insects forms congregate along the reeds, grasses, and water weeds growing at the edges. It's like an entomologic zoo. Prominent are the predatory larvae of the dragonfly and damselfly, a large group of aquatic beetles, the boatmen or backswimmers, and higher on the evolutionary ladder, crayfish and tadpoles, etc. Certain larval and pupal forms hatch, too, by simply crawling out of the water onto a grass or reed stem rather than bursting dramatically through the surface film. If you spot fish in close to the bank, it's a fair bet that they're feeding, surface rises or no. It's good news, since you can concentrate your efforts in a fairly small and select part of the pond. Casts are shorter, too, and rather than having to throw the opaque line across the surface, it can be draped unobtrusively over bankside vegetation.

Another good bet is to explore the deepest portions. Trout will congregate there because of enhanced cover. During the heat of summer this should also be the coolest water. As a rule we assume that a lake's deepest part will be out near the center. It's not necessarily that way with beaverponds. Quite often the lodge or house will be near the center, forming an island. The

water just off the dam face in an actively maintained pond is usually one of the deepest areas, but check the perimeter, too. Just as in sluggish, ponded portions of a stream, the slightest wisp of current is worth finding, since it will collect food. Look for a feeble current trail by following floating objects as they make their way slowly toward the lip of the dam. In small ponds with a defined inflow I draw an imaginary line from that point toward the center of the dam where the outflow should be. This line may or may not cross the center of the pond and often describes the original channel of the watercourse before it was dammed. That old channel should be the deepest part of the pond, and if not silted in sometimes forms a reef via its submerged banks. As lake fishers know, those reefs abound with insect life.

Stalking Ponds

Getting into position to cast without spooking a pond is awfully difficult when the water is crystal-clear and slick. Stalking-horse cover objects such as willow clumps are occasionally helpful, and so is a low profile, as in duck walking. Even then you may be foiled by bank "shuggles" or the "jello tremor." Rather than being made of honest dirt, the banks are a soggy conglomerate of rotting sticks, grass roots, and water held tenuously together by just a bit of mud. It's like walking on a grassy mattress and bedsprings. The merest vibration gets transmitted way out into the pond. One firm step is enough to turn off feeding fish, so it's a matter of trying to locomote via careful shuffling. Actually, shuffling is not a bad idea in the interest of avoiding another sort of pitfall. I refer to those grass-disguised holes and channels that are so common in beaverland. They are very much like miniature elephant traps (as I imagine elephant traps). I've seen companions disappear with great suddenness and finality when they had been walking just a few yards ahead only seconds before. (This calamity is followed by beaver-damning.) It can be a good ploy to stand just at the base or foot of the dam, casting over it. Vibrations aren't an issue, and there's not much of you to stick up into the trouts' windows. Watch the current at the dam's lip, though, lest

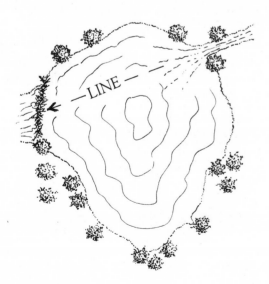

Current trail between inlet and dam.

Casting over the dam. Safe footing plus a low profile.

it catch your back line and weave it through the maze of snags from which dams are constructed. (A longer rod is most helpful.) I'd generally discourage wading out into these ponds. "Mucking" is a better term than wading, for if there is anything in the world that the word muck describes, it's the bottom of a beaverpond. Webster defines muck as "slimy dirt or filth," so I may exaggerate slightly, but still, muck is muck. You can get mired so deeply and quickly that horrible thoughts of quicksand flood the mind. Beyond this, all sorts of silt gets stirred up to diffuse throughout the pond, thus announcing a foreign presence. The same is true of surface disturbance rings.

Presentations

If the pond covers an acre or so and the fish are working well out, the flyrodder is in trouble unless the water is cloudy or the surface is riffled. The problem is the coarse flyline. No matter if it is a tapered 3-weight, that line will make a commotion when it comes down and cast a shadow on the bottom, too, if there is sun. In this special circumstance I think spinning gear can be an advantage. Distance is never a problem, and gossamer monofilament wafts down ever so gently, sinks, and casts little shadow. As to the bubble or casting weight, it's usually possible to throw it well past and to one side of the target area. With patience the fly will drift naturally into the preferred water, perhaps aided by a stealthy turn or two of the reel. Dry flies can be presented via a series of gradually lengthening casts. With wets you can make the same presentation, either allowing the fly to drift toward the dam or retrieving it parallel to the face.

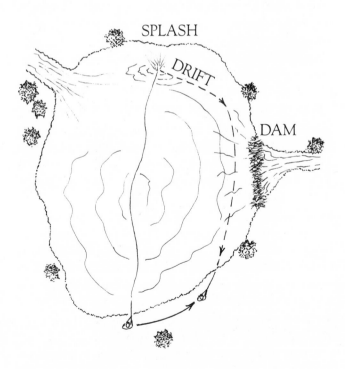

Spin casting is helpful when a pond is large and still.

Fly Types

I prefer sunken flies for pond fishing. Whereas a floating fly creates an unsightly wake when it is pulled across the surface, a wet fly does not. Thus one can troll a sunken lure from the far point of the cast back to the angler's position. Since the fly covers or passes through a much larger amount of water in a shorter period than a fly drifting on the surface, more fish have a chance to notice it. It's frustrating to watch a becalmed dry fly sitting out there hopelessly like a tiny sailboat waiting for some breeze. I do remember a few instances when grasshoppers were afloat in late season when it was fun to actively retrieve a floating fly, leaving a wake quite on purpose. A sinking fly pulls its leader down behind it, avoiding shadows that leaders sitting in the surface film cast across the bottom. Wet flies can suggest a tremendous variety of food forms and can be offered in so many ways. The angler has unlimited opportunity to exercise his imagination. They can be crawled ever so slowly across a silty bottom, kicking up little puffs in the manner of a creeping caddis. They can be swum in a smooth, steady manner or with little jerks and darts, shrimp-like, or in the manner of a dragonfly nymph. You can fish a wet just beneath the surface or even on the underside of the surface film when trout are taking larvae in that very special layer. Tiny wet flies are sometimes very important in beaverponding. Diptera or midge species are especially common, and larvae of many aquatic beetles also tend toward the petite. Very simple patterns such as a Grey Hackle Peacock are a good bet. Fly weighting isn't often needed, and this is one situation in which I like a delicate sinking line, say a 3- or 4-weight double taper in some somber hue. Oddly though, when the sun is bright and there's a breeze, beaverpond trout will sometimes take a dry fly better than a wet. I think it's because they get too good a look at the sunken fly. When the surface film becomes a tossing blanket of molten silver, I'd guess that a floating fly is just a dark blob with the tips of the hackle and tails showing through.

When planning to fish these ponds, there is no finer weather than a grey, misting rain. A gentle drizzle gives you excellent cover, meanwhile cooling and oxygenating the water. Theoretically and reasonably these conditions invigorate the trout and the insect life within the pond. Low light conditions as at dusk also correlate with increased feeding activity. In going back over many years' worth of beaverpond fishing, it is amazing to find that almost without exception the best days were either on the rainy side or included the last hour or so of light.

I have a certain ambivalency about beaverponding. I could never become an addict. The kaleidoscopic change that comes with following a creek's channel is too much a part of my fishing. A running water pathway is sprinkled with way stations, each posing a new and distinctive angling problem. Still, when you meet a pond there is the opportunity to try a different kind of angling. And when really large trout are caught in small stream systems, a beaverpond with just the right set of qualities is usually involved. We owe the beaver a further debt for creating fishing where there could be none otherwise.

10
In Final Analysis

Flyfishing is a neat, clean word, but those ten letters hardly describe a single activity, for flyfishing encompasses a whole menagerie of sub-hobbies. Included are fly tying, rod building, tackle collecting, entomology, competitive flycasting, trophy fishing, and many others. Those facets that shine brightest for one angler are unlikely to be the same that captivate another, but an angler can wed several of these splinters off the sport without committing any culpable form of bigamy. Indeed most of us are polygamous in this respect. An appreciation of the distinctive intimacy of small trout-streams is still another side. Those of us who fit that mold regard adjustments of technique and tackle as interesting expansions of our sport. By contrast, I know many dedicated flyfishers who are just as preoccupied with "big." They want to catch big trout on big water using big casts made with big rods and so on. There's nothing wrong with this. "Big" is merely a style and a preference. I count myself lucky, since I spend fully half my angling time on sizable rivers and am invariably happy just to be out on trout water of any dimension. One thing's certain, you can't equate a stream's size with the overall difficulty of the fishing problems that it poses. I freely admit that there are creeks filled with trout whose naivete and desire to compete with their fellows for our flies is remarkable. If reasonably open of bank, these fisheries are ideal for the beginner. At the other extreme are those small waters that demand special skills and tackle modifications. There we find the sort of abstruse pleasure that comes with mastering a difficult challenge. Between these extremes there's a whole spectrum of relative difficulty.

No matter the caliber of the water, reading is a required skill. Here the creek offers an advantage for the beginner. Although the filagree of features that makes up a creek's text is finely drawn, seen up close there is greater definition of detail than we find in rivers. Stalking might be regarded as a picky exercise. It takes time, requires patience and concentration. Yet stalking brings one into a kind of intimate contact with a stream. It's like getting on all fours to plant or weed a garden. Stalking is an attitude sort of thing, and so is the willingness to fool with the funny casts that go with fishing small streams. Some are sufficiently peculiar as to be considered unnatural. And for a person who is accustomed to rivers, tooling up for creek fishing amounts to a major shift in gears. The tendency is to pick a rod that's too short. And the soft action that's so nice for tight-quarters casting must seem uncomfortable too. Neither are long-range flycasters accustomed to line overloading or to short leaders with fine tippets.

Temper control is another critical asset. This is every bit as vital in creekcraft as on the golf course. You don't really learn the value of something until you lose it. On this basis I can claim some knowledge of temper, both on the links and astream. During the latter part of my youth I suffered from the misconception that I could become a scratch handicapper, even a pro. I learned in the process just what golf and temper have to do with one another. It's quite a bit. Those of us who have gotten involved with the little white ball know that the angrier a golfer becomes, the worse he plays. It's the classic vicious circle. There's a parallel with casting flies down the narrow, watery fairways of small troutstreams, fringed by a special brand of rough. Just as the golfer may hit his ball into thick grass, the woods, sand or water hazards, so may our flies alight in tall conifers and other unseemly places. Wouldn't you agree that missing a three-foot putt is analogous to messing up a short, simple cast into a sure target? Experience, skill, and caution will reduce the frequency of mishaps, but they are still going to occur. These entanglements waste time, ruin good water, and invariably result in the loss of some leaders and flies. Meanwhile, the deerfly bites, invisible sentinels ruin prime targets, and so on. As these misadventures mount up during the day I used to become increasingly testy and less rather than more careful. Admitting that I once threw my rod way up on the bank (another analogy to golf), there is a psychological gam-

bit that I've found soothing: simply, I've learned to expect a certain number of hangups. I anticipate them, not with joy perhaps, but with a certain resignation. I tell myself that the finest golfers hit some bad shots during most rounds. If you can sell yourself this bill of goods I believe you'll come out ahead. Thus when the fly comes to roost irretrievably midst a cluster of pine cones high above, just look up at the pretty blue sky as you snap the leader and smile (wanly perhaps). You might even chuckle, "Well, that was long overdue."

The fishers of small streams has a unique opportunity to build courage and character. In order to get the most out of nook-and-cranny angling, it's necessary to take a few chances. The catch that I remember best came from an almost impossible hide on Trout Creek near Colorado Springs. In one spot the water hugged the face of a high bluff that forced the channel into a tight zigzag. The creek was so swallowed up in willows that it disappeared, as if drained by their thirsty roots. One day I edged my way around the first right-angle bend and was suddenly waist deep in a pothole of cold water. It occurred to me that if Trout Creek held any outsize fish, one of them should make this bower his

Small streams are special for many reasons.

abode. Getting a fly into this spot was another matter. Dapping from either bank was impossible due to the willows, and the tight Z bend precluded floating a fly down from above. Facing upstream, my backcast was hampered by cottonwoods. Worse, the hole was protected by a curtain of merging willow fronds. The only chink in this green armor was a window gap some four feet across and just above water level. On my next trip I tried a roll cast, but the loop was too wide and I hung up. On my way home that evening, I worked the backcast between boughs of the cottonwoods, sidearm. The cast seemed just short, as if the fly might not drop far enough over the "sill" to reach the water. Then suddenly the willow fronds slashed downward midst wild splashings. Thanks to a great deal of luck I eventually landed a thick-bodied, 16-inch brown, my finest trout ever from this stream. I looked forward to future peeks through this window, but to no avail. When I did manage to drop the fly in, no one was home. That little pool had probably been the sanctum of this senior citizen for a long time. I'm sorry I killed that exceptional fish. I had no good reason to do so, and I robbed myself of the fun of trying to fool the big guy a second time.

Most of this book has been devoted to ways and means of catching trout with no comment about what to do next. I find it difficult to push "catch and release" without sounding sanctimonious. Those of us who love small streams don't need to be reminded about conservation anyway. What about creeks that are over-populated with stunted fish? Is it really wrong to take out a limit? Might not the fishery actually profit from pruning? My attitude was colored by the following experience: Years ago we packed into the South Fork of the White River in northwestern Colorado each summer. Within the valley we found a short canyon, cut like a trench through a granite outcropping. The canyon was almost impassable, but its terracing pools were filled with beautiful rainbow/cutthroat hybrids. Once we discovered the place, it became everyone's favorite. There was reason to believe that members of our party were the only visitors to this wild canyon. Nonetheless, we managed to virtually fish it out over the course of just ten summers! We turned what had been a hot spot into a sterile quarter mile of river. I have no idea how long that little canyon took to recover, if it ever did. Smaller streams are just that much more susceptible to thoughtless harvesting. I feel particularly protective toward our native cutthroat. They require the coldest, purest water we have left and soon lose their identity when they cross with rainbow, as is their tendency in mixed populations. Fortunately, attitudes toward the killing of fish have changed since I was a youngster. Those were cornucopia days with seemingly endless supplies of trout. Resorts and fishing camps typically displayed pictures of clients with huge strings of fish dangling from a taut rope like pickets in a fence. Back then a boy was expected to display his catch as tangible proof of his prowess. It was a demonstration of manly accomplishment, and I'm afraid that it was almost fatal for any trout to be caught by me. They went into my creel like so many merit badges. With three fishing sons in our family, the rule has been that your claim is your catch, no questions asked. Besides, freezer-stored trout soon acquire the taste of wet Kleenex.

A net is helpful both in capturing and freeing trout with a minimum of harm, but nets are a nuisance when working brushy creeks. The elastic cord is virtually an anti-personnel device aimed at the back of your head. I concentrate instead on keeping my fingers out of gill slits, avoiding undue pressure on the rib cage, and nursing tired trout back to life. Beyond question barbless hooks help in returning a fish as quickly as possible and with a minimum of handling. Many anglers are reluctant to go barbless for fear of losing too many fish. I once became curious enough about this question to conduct a series of experiments. I've found that the percentage of hooked fish that I eventually land on small streams is almost identical, barbed versus barbless. The only difference has been a slightly higher strike to hook ratio fishing barbless, same pattern and hook caliber. It's worth it though, particularly with larger hooks such as the #6s we use for stone fly imitations and streamers. Armed with a barb these create vicious wounds.

In closing I want to comment on the real value of some form of log. A fishing diary hardly qualifies as an item of equipment, yet I almost think of my log as if it were a piece of tackle. I refer to it by habit when preparing to fish a stream that I've worked before. Almost invariably I find valuable notations that can be turned to practical advantage. These may concern weather or water conditions for a given date, information about prevalent insects and their activities, fly patterns that were and were not effective, modes of presentation that worked or did not, etc., etc. It's surprising how many of these important details I would otherwise forget. It's also great fun to relive certain trips months or years later through this handwritten chronicle. It's a way of recapturing at least a whiff of the experience for posterity. The half hour or so that I spend filling in my log after a day on the stream seems well worthwhile.

Creekcraft is special because of the intimacy between the angler and his surroundings. With everything close at hand and reduced in scale, it's an elbow-rubbing relationship. For me this is the warp and woof of creekcraft. Small streams have been outstanding teachers in my personal faculty of fisheries. I feel especially fortunate that my satisfaction and pleasure have little to do with size of the waters that I fish. I hope it can be that way for you too.

Index